THE Smarter PHYSICIAN

CONQUERING YOUR PRACTICE'S BILLING AND REIMBURSEMENT

Bhagwan Satiani, MD, MBA, FACS

Production Credits
Editorial Director: Marilee E. Aust
Project Editor: Anne Serrano, MA
Page Design, Composition, and Production: Glacier Publishing Services, Inc.
Copy Editor: Alys Novak, MBA, Discovery Communications
Proofreader: Glacier Publishing Services, Inc.
Cover Design: Ian Serff, Serff Creative Group, Inc.

MGMA Information Center Subcommittee
Chair: Charles D. Moses, FACMPE
Samantha Kempster, MBA, CMPE
Carolyn Pickles, MBA, FACMPE
Mary Pat Whaley, FACMPE

Library of Congress Cataloging-in-Publication Data
Satiani, Bhagwan.
   The smarter physician. Conquering your practice's billing and reimbursement / by Bhagwan Satiani.
     p. ; cm.
   Includes bibliographical references and index.
   Summary: "This book, a tool for practice managers and physicians, dissects the nuts and bolts of a medical practice. Among other topics, the book reviews the revenue cycle, reimbursement, billing, and cost/volume/profit analysis; shows how Medicare measures clinical activity; and discusses pay for performance"--Provided by publisher.
   ISBN 978-1-56829-286-1
   1. Medical fees. 2. Health insurance claims--Data processing. 3. Medicine--Practice--Accounting. 4. Medicine--Practice--Finance. 5. Medical offices--Management. I. Medical Group Management Association. II. Title. III. Title: Conquering your practice's billing and reimbursement.
   [DNLM: 1. Financial Management--organization & administration--United States. 2. Patient Credit and Collection--organization & administration--United States. 3. Insurance Claim Reporting--United States. 4. Insurance, Health, Reimbursement--United States. 5. Practice Management, Medical--organization & administration--United States. W 80 S253sc 2007]
R728.5.S248 2007
368.38'20068--dc22

                                   2007020114

Item #6798
ISBN: 978-1-56829-286-1

Printed in the United States of America
10 9 8 7 6 5 4 3 2 1

The Smarter Physician Series

Volume 1
Demystifying the Business of Medicine in Your Practice

Volume 2
Conquering Your Practice's Billing and Reimbursement

Volume 3
Investing in Your Personal Financial Health

Dedication

I am eternally grateful to God for linking my life to this great country, the United States of America. My ever-lasting gratitude goes to my parents, Sobhraj and Lachmi Satiani, for the foundation of patience, self-reliance, and trust in God. My children, Anmol, Anand, and Nidhi, deserve a special thank you for their constant doting love, support, and encouragement. Finally, I am blessed to have the ideal friend, wife, and companion for more than 36 years who has been a pillar of strength and given me the freedom to indulge and follow my dreams. Thank you, Mira.

Acknowledgments

I am very grateful to all the contributing authors for the hard work in writing their chapters on time and responding to many requests for clarification. Their expertise and real-world experience has added immensely to this work. Many individuals helped in many ways during the process of writing the three volumes in The Smarter Physician Series. My sincere thanks to: Anmol Satiani and Anand Satiani for proofreading and insightful comments; Todd Wheeler for a helpful critique of the chapter on compensation; Chris Kaiser and Ray Manley for help with use of relative value units and department policies; Steve LeClair and Howard Pirwitz with UBS for generous assistance with several chapters on finance; to Charlie Black, Lee Miller, and Ron Ohsner with HRH for their insights into professional liability insurance; to Nate Goldberg for suggesting changes in the chapters on life and disability insurance; to Tim Nagy for a review of the tax status of hospitals; to Chester Krisiewicz and Loribeth Bethel for advice on taxation topics; to Asim Sheikh with UBS for his critique of chapters on stocks, mutual funds, and bonds; and Phil Heit for educating me on book publishing. I would like to thank my friend and colleague, Pat Vaccaro (Division of Vascular Surgery), and Chris Ellison (department chair), for their support as well as Wiley "Chip" Souba, our dean at The Ohio State University College of Medicine for encouraging me and promptly agreeing to write a chapter. Finally, my gratitude to a very hard-working, patient editor assigned by MGMA: Bob Redling. Thank you, Bob.

Also appreciated is the assistance from MGMA's Information Center staff including Marilee Aust, Editorial Director; Anne Serrano, Information Products Manager; and Alys Novak, copy editor.

Contents

List of Tables

List of Figures

Introduction

Generations of physicians have practiced medicine with pride and have been able to maintain a disconnect between the economic and the clinical aspects of medicine. Some practitioners continue to insist that the practice of medicine is simply healing the sick and that the business side will take care of itself.

That may have been true in years past. The fact is, being better versed in the economic side of medicine and providing the best and most compassionate care are not mutually exclusive. The two are perfectly compatible. Indeed, in this era, the physician must make good business decisions in order to provide uncompensated care that is part of all physicians' responsibility to society. Even a decade ago, operating margins were generous enough to allow physicians to be inattentive to the business side of the practice and still be able to make a good living, provide charity care, give office staff well-deserved benefits, and pay malpractice premiums. Not any more.

The Accreditation Council for Graduate Medical Education (ACGME), which is responsible for the accreditation of post-medical school training in the United States, has issued a new initiative called "Educating Physicians for the 21st Century" that recognizes the importance of addressing a serious deficiency in training programs.[1] The ACGME has identified six general competencies for medical residency programs, one of which is "Systems-Based Practice." This competency calls for educating residents in the economics of health care systems, billing, coding, and patient safety.[2]

As the senior physician in my practice, I was expected to know everything ranging from office hiring procedures to personal finance in guiding junior associates. With no background in the economic side of medicine and a 20-something secretary with no business or management experience, I believe I have made every mistake managing a practice that is possible—and survived!

Physicians are taught little to nothing in medical school or their residency about the non-clinical aspect of medicine. (See Table I.1 for a review of the knowledge base needed for accomplishing tasks during a medical career.) Basic information about how and where to look for a successful practice,

Table I.1   Knowledge Base Needed for Accomplishing Tasks During a Medical Career

Career Stages	Task	Knowledge Needed
Residency	Attending presence for services, E&M codes	Billing/coding/fraud and abuse
	Dealing with pharmaceutical companies/vendors	Ethical guidelines
	Dealing with mal-occurrences in patient care	Malpractice, litigation
	Looking for a job	Contract negotiations
	Assessing a buy-in	Valuation of practice
	Interviewing, negotiating signing bonus, moving expenses	Anti-kickback regulations, fraud and abuse regulations, compensation
Practice	Starting practice	Basic accounting/finance/corporations/tax structure, payment systems
	Hiring/firing staff	Human resources
	Pursuing academic practice	Stark laws relating to academic medical centers, practice plans, contract negotiations
	Having a successful practice	Marketing, cost–volume–profit analysis, budgets, financial ratios
	Ensuring professional liability understood	Medico-legal knowledge, professional liability insurance, National Practitioner Data Bank, expert witness role
	Ensuring health, disability/life insurance issues covered	Health/disability/life insurance
	Saving for children's education	Forms of trusts, educational savings account
	Having a pension plan	Regulations, retirement plans
	Performing as a hospital director	Structure of not-for-profits, Stark/anti-kickback regulations, physician–hospital relations
	Leasing space from hospital, leasing space to hospital and others	Anti-kickback regulations, Stark laws
	Investing	Finance, stocks/bonds/fixed investments, taxable and non-taxable investments, trusts, savings programs
	Opening outpatient facility	Joint ventures, accounting, finance, Stark law
	Helping hospital with efficiency program	Gainsharing, pay-for-performance programs
	Billing	Reimbursement issues, Medicare, private insurers, mechanics of billing/coding/ revenue cycle/False Claims Act
End of practice	Selling practice	Valuation of practice
	Retiring	Retirement planning, Medicare
	Becoming a physician executive, looking for part-time employment	Physician–executive transformation, contract negotiations, business schools

what to ask in an interview, how to spot problems in an employment opportunity, and be aware of the value of the financial package being offered (other than the salary) is woefully inadequate. Any useful information from other residents is mixed with either outdated or inaccurate data so as to render it less than valuable. New physicians are then expected to start by hiring the most valuable commodity in a practice: a good business manager. The expectation is that they will match their skill in patient care with being financially successful. In an era of group practices, they rely on their senior colleagues to manage the business side. The likelihood that the senior colleagues have any formal education or training in this area is slim. All decisions are based on personal experience, "we have always done it this way," or total reliance on advice from their accountants, attorneys, and financial advisors. By the time a junior physician discovers that he/she made a mistake understanding what was really in the contract, that the balance sheet of the hiring entity was a disaster, the retirement plan was inadequate, the financial advisor was not honest, and that the billing practices were illegal, valuable time has been wasted.

The urge to learn and then teach younger physicians about the business side of medicine made me realize that there was room for a resource that physicians could refer to and read about basic business topics valuable in a medical practice. This book started out as a small manual for residents, to be given out as reference material in business/practice management classes. The current form has been made possible by all the contributors who have labored over their assignments with no expectation other than to help with the education process of the all-important business managers for existing practices, future physicians, and current practitioners who desire to gain enough knowledge to ask the right questions of their professional advisors. It is my hope that this book serves as a stimulus to learn much more than the small slice of knowledge that this book offers. Undoubtedly, there will be mistakes and omissions that come with a first attempt at organizing a project such as this.

Conquering Your Practice's Billing and Reimbursement, the second volume of The Smarter Physician Series, dissects the nuts and bolts of a medical practice.

Part One: From Paperwork to Payment: Solving the Mystery starts with some pointers on the revenue cycle by long-term administrator Ray Manley (chapter 1). Important steps toward comprehending the complexities of reimbursement are covered in chapter 2 (The Private Insurance System) and chapter 3 (How Medicare Works). In chapter 4, Rebecca

Dawson, an experienced coding specialist, breaks down the individual components of evaluation, management, modifiers, and other aspects of billing (Getting Paid, Part 1: Introduction to Coding and the Global Surgery Package). For physicians in both private and academic practices, chapter 5, on how Medicare actually measures clinical activity provides a basic grounding in this enigma (Getting Paid, Part 2: The Resource-Based Relative Value Scale [RBRVS], Medicare Physician Fee Schedule and Other Payment Mechanisms).

In Part Two: A Guide to Accounting and Finance, E. Ann Gabriel puts her knowledge of accounting and finance to work in two very important and readable chapters on financial statements—What They Are and What They Tell Us (chapter 6) and Using Financial Statements to Make Decisions (chapter 7)—that serve as the basis for understanding financial statements and profitability ratios. Cost/volume/profit analysis, addressed in chapter 8 (Measuring Profit and Loss: The Rules of Cost and Volume Measurement), assists the reader in challenging assumptions about services that may or may not be profitable for medical practices.

Part Three: Physician Compensation is intended to start a conversation about compensation and the current hot-button issue of pay for performance. Physician compensation is a complicated issue, and chapter 9 (Models, Methods, and Philosophies) and chapter 10 (Pay for Performance: A Work in Progress) serve as a good beginning for the inquisitive reader.

As an extra value, the book contains a CD with additional material, including a glossary and a list of financial information and health care law Websites, as well as other valuable resources.

References

1. Accreditation Council for Graduate Medical Education, www.acgme.org (accessed May 23, 2006).

2. B. Joyce, "Introduction to Competency-based Education, Facilitator's Guide" ACGME (April 2006) www.acgme.org/outcome/e-learn/21M1_facmanual.pdf (accessed May 23, 2006).

Part 1

From Paperwork to Payment

Chapter 1

The Revenue Cycle

Ray Manley, CMPE

The revenue cycle is most simply defined as the step-by-step process of converting a patient service to practice revenue. Sounds simple enough, and in many respects it is not a difficult process. However, as anyone who has purchased a product promising "simple assembly instructions included" knows, following each step in the exact order is the only way the product looks and functions as intended.

So it is with the revenue cycle. One step flows naturally to the next and all are dependent on each other. Shortcuts inevitably cause a disruption in the process, resulting in additional work effort, strained patient relations, and lost revenue. Just as we often hear successful players and coaches in the sports world demanding an emphasis on mastering the fundamentals, so must we follow and master the fundamentals in the revenue cycle.

Knowledge and skill are the products the physician brings to the patient. The revenue, or fee, received is the payment for that knowledge and skill. The first cannot continue in the absence of the second. A solid financial foundation is a non-negotiable factor in any successful practice. Following a comprehensive and practical plan of action will help ensure positive results.

Components of the Revenue Cycle

The revenue cycle is often diagrammed in great detail with every minute component defined and analyzed. There is certainly a place for such an in-depth study, but for now we will concentrate on the fundamentals of the revenue cycle, which are:

- Payer contracting;
- Appointment scheduling;
- Preregistration;
- Registration;
- HIPAA information for patients;

- Coding/charge capture;

- Insurance/patient billing;

- Accounts receivable follow-up; and

- Benchmarking.

As we briefly discuss these components, the purpose is to provide an overview and encourage interest. Other writers have devoted entire books to many of these individual components. There is a great deal of detailed study available for those in the practice responsible for these functions. As a physician, you need not concern yourself with the multitude of details, but it is imperative that you be aware of the revenue cycle's components and insist that each is getting appropriate attention.

Payer Contracting

Payer contracting was not a significant issue until the late 1980s. Until then, only government programs, Blue Cross and Blue Shield, and a few major employers had contractual or participation agreements in place. Reimbursement was reasonable, and the rules were not particularly onerous.

Then the commercial insurance carriers' managed care model took hold on the West Coast and moved eastward. Where government programs provided some reimbursement for patients with little or no existing coverage or money, managed care replaced the excellent reimbursement of commercial plans with significantly reduced fixed fees in return for directing volumes of patients to the participating practice. Of course, because almost all providers signed up, volume did not really go up, but payments surely went down.

As a result, regardless of size, participating practices must:

- Review and understand the contracts they sign. These contracts are written by and for the benefit of the insurance company, so don't be surprised that they are tilted in the insurer's favor;

- Analyze the fees they will be paying for your services. This information is often difficult to get, but at the very least insist on knowing the allowance fees for the services and procedures that make up the majority of your claims activity;

- Estimate of the volume of business this contract will direct to your practice. If it is a relatively insignificant amount, perhaps agreeing to substantial discounts is not in your best interests. Conversely, having too high a percentage of your potential practice revenue tied up in one contract could present major cash flow problems if the contract terminates; and

- Inquire about termination and renewal provisions. Must the contract be renewed annually? How often are rates adjusted up, or down? What are the termination provisions? Can the insurance company terminate with a 30-day notice, but you must wait 180 days to terminate? Remember, they wrote the rules.

Appointment Scheduling

Appointment scheduling, along with the next two sections dealing with preregistration and registration are, in many respects, one topic. But, because each has a specific function, we will deal with them as independent subjects.

The appointment scheduling system must be:

- Automated so that the practice can take advantage of the wealth of information being gathered. Custom reporting can provide valuable demographic data, produce no-show reports, perform automated appointment reminders, and so on;

- User-friendly, not only to the staff member booking appointments, but also if consideration is given to allowing patients to book their own appointments or otherwise access the system; and

- Linked to the billing system to ensure the capture of all patient charges.

Preregistration

Preregistration, or *short-form registration*, as it is sometimes called, has several significant objectives. In addition to establishing a new patient file, it provides an opportunity to update some key information for existing patients. Ideally, this occurs up to one week prior to the appointment. This function allows the practice to:

- Review and update basic information to ensure the practice has the patient's current home address, employer, and insurance information;

- Verify insurance coverage and confirm that the service to be performed is eligible for payment;

- Check for secondary insurance or other sources of payment such as auto liability, workers' compensation, etc.;

- Check for pending claims, and to determine if there are unpaid balances due from previous patient encounters; and

- Request that the patient bring current insurance cards and a means of paying past-due amounts and any current obligations.

Registration

When the patient arrives for the appointment and the preregistration process has been completed as needed, there should only be a few administrative matters to attend to:

- Complete the registration form and update any new or changed information;

- Provide the patient with a HIPAA (Health Insurance Portability and Accountability Act) notice of privacy practices for information and signature;

- Review financial policies of the practice if necessary; and

- Collect any past due balances, deductibles, and copays.

This last step—collection—provides an opportunity that should not be missed. It is the most opportune time to ask for payment. The patient payment obligation may be significantly greater than the available insurance coverage; so collecting at registration can produce immediate cash income to the practice and eliminate the added cost of follow-up billing.

HIPAA Information for Patients

Informing patients about how the medical practice protects their confidential medical information and under which conditions it discloses that information is a critical step. Also important is paying careful attention to the design of the reception area and the behavior of those who work there. Avoid breaches of HIPAA-protected patient health information by warning staff not to discuss patients in hallways, restrooms, or other public areas within earshot of other patients. Few physician medical practices have the space for semi-private cubicles for patient registration as seen in hospitals, but careful attention to information gathering and dissemination can avoid most security lapses. Paperwork with identifiable patient information should not be kept on or near public counters. Computer screens and printer and fax output trays should be positioned where they cannot be easily seen by others. While it would not be a problem in many practices to ask for patients' names on a sign-in sheet, asking them to describe their medical complaints could be considered a violation of privacy.

Charge Posting and Coding

Although the previous steps have prepared the way, the completion of the patient's current episode of care formally begins the process of converting service to revenue.

Even the most basic practice management or billing system is capable of some remarkable functions. There is also the option of outsourcing this or other functions of the revenue cycle. However, whether any of the functions are performed in-house or outsourced, the same concerns and obligations apply.

Specifically, the following must be considered.

- Maintain an up-to-date charge master (a central repository of charges and associated coding information in either printed or software format), which should contain:
  - Narrative descriptions of services;
  - Current Procedural Terminology (CPT®) codes;
  - Fees;
  - Relative value units (total, work, or both); and
  - Location of service (hospital, office, or other).

Updates to these data should occur annually, preferably the first of each year to coincide with the release of new, deleted, or revised codes in American Medical Association's CPT listing.

Whether or not physicians assign their own CPT billing codes, a qualified coder (preferably certified) should review or assign all codes before the claim is billed. Billing is a complicated process that, when performed correctly, can have an impact on the speed and amount of payment. If done poorly, coding can not only delay payment, but also lead to legal issues, refunds, and penalties.

It is important to ensure that charges for all services are at the proper levels and that they, and the location of service, are entered into the billing system. There are many electronic and manual systems available to track services and billing. It is well worth the effort to ensure that this is done on a daily basis.

Insurance Billing

At this point, the service has been rendered and the required information to file a claim with a third-party payer is in the system and ready to go.

The goal now is to get an accurate "clean claim" to the payer as quickly as possible.

Several simple steps to accomplish a clean claim should have already occurred. They include:

- Verification of coverage;

- Obtaining of required signatures;

- Capture of all charges;

- Accurate coding of the service; and

- Creation of the account in the billing system.

Before releasing the claim for billing, these additional steps should be considered:

- Use pre-billing edit software to review your claims for missing information or easily corrected errors before they leave your office. An outdated CPT code, or a code that suggests something medically inconsistent (for example, a female-related procedure performed on a male), will result in a denial that will cause delay in payment and additional work for your staff;

- Follow the payer's rules. There is a contract that sets forth your obligations as well as theirs. Your staff should be aware of special billing requirements;

- Make use of electronic billing, and the electronic posting of payments when available. It is fast, efficient, and accurate; and

- Cross-reference payments received with the contract. Are you getting the correct amount? If not, contact the payer representative, or file an appeal.

Accounts Receivable Follow-Up

Often the claim is filed and payment is made in a remarkably fast and efficient manner. A clean claim filed and processed electronically often goes unnoticed because it requires little, if any, attention. Unfortunately, a practice cannot simply depend on this occurring on all claims.

A structured, systematic system must be in place to follow-up problem accounts in a timely, consistent manner. Steps to consider include:

- Developing work files based on predetermined parameters. Typically, your staff should work higher balance accounts first. These may be arranged by payer, physician, length of time elapsed since billing, or other criterion;

- Developing a list of staff contacts at the various payers who have been helpful or have the authority to cut through red tape;

- Reviewing amounts owed by patients. Even if their obligations only represent a small portion of your accounts receivable, these could add up to a substantial dollar amount;

- Giving payments the same amount of attention and swift action for posting as is given to submitting charges. Internal controls must be in place to ensure prompt posting and balancing of payments to protect the accuracy of record-keeping and the practice income;

- Monitoring contractual adjustments. The amounts that your practice agrees to write off are your discounts to the payer. A monitoring system will ensure that these discounts are accurate and not being allowed improperly. The system also ensures that the discounts are not being allowed just because doing so provides a convenient way to close an account. Discounts and write-offs are prime areas involved in many theft situations; and

- Returning refunds promptly. They are not the property of the practice and must be returned without delay. A high credit balance artificially lowers accounts receivable totals and may mask a serious follow-up problem. Government payers and courts consider retaining refunds for extended periods of time to be a fraud and abuse issue.

Benchmarking: Key Indicators to Watch

Effectively performing all of the required steps in the revenue cycle should result in a practice that enjoys a strong financial foundation. However, even smooth-running organizations have areas for improvement. These potential opportunities may be easily identified by benchmarking key indicators to industry standards, such as those available from the Medical Group Management Association, specialty societies, and so forth.

Some benchmarks of interest are discussed in the following sections.

Collection Rates

At one time, the *gross collection rate* was a key metric, but in these days of high contractual adjustments and fixed payments, it has lost much of its value. Instead, the *net collection rate* should be measured. The formula is simple: charges less contractual adjustments divided by collections.

Figure 1.1   Billing/Collection Ratios

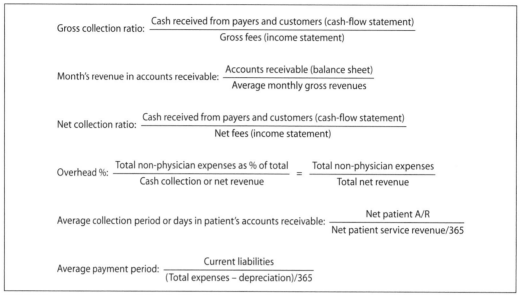

NOTE: This figure appears as Appendix C on the CD so that you can use it as a template.

Although the goal should be a 100-percent collection rate, most practices experience acceptable levels in the high 90 percentile. (See Figure 1.1 for billing and collection ratios.)

Days in Accounts Receivable

Days in accounts receivable represents the number of days worth of charges in the practice's accounts receivable file waiting for payment. Most organizations that report this item consider a range of 40 days to 60 days acceptable. The practice must be the final judge because the mix of payers in the practice greatly influences this measure. A practice with a high Medicare utilization rate may have very low days, while another handling a large volume of trauma may have higher days.

Percent of Accounts Receivable over 90 Days

Balances in the category of *percent of accounts receivable over 90 days* should be kept to a minimum. To be in this category, something has caused a delay that is almost twice the norm of a clean claim. The practice's claims follow-up staff needs to determine the cause of the delay and resolve it quickly.

Charge Lag Time

Charge lag time shows how long it is taking from the time a billable patient service is provided to the time that claim is sent to the insurance carrier for payment. Each practice is different, but the obvious answer here is the quicker, the better.

Denial Rates

Insurance carriers deny claims for a multitude of reasons. These *denial rates* need to be researched, corrected, and re-billed or appealed promptly. Keep in mind, the problem could be in the practice, such as using outdated CPT codes, or incorrect locations of service.

Collections per Relative Value Unit

Collections per relative value unit (RVU) is an alternative way to measure collections. Most billing systems can track total or work RVUs, so collections may be divided by either measure, at the discretion of the practice, and monitored over time. This not only measures collections in general, but can also show improvements related to better contracting techniques with payers.

Overhead Cost

There are numerous ways to measure the cost of doing business in a practice. These expenses must be reviewed to identify those that can be reduced or eliminated. Some areas of *overhead cost* such as rent and staff salaries in high-cost geographic locations seem to defy control. Many of the better-performing practices report higher overhead dollars spent, but more dollars brought into the practice. Scrimping on staffing is not the answer to controlling overhead. The focus should be on controlling those expenses that can be controlled, and converting more patient services to dollars collected.

Conclusion

The steps in the revenue cycle are not difficult, but all demand attention. A competent, well-trained staff is essential, and oversight of each step is mandatory. Several professional medical management associations and specialty societies publish excellent survey reports that can be used to develop the necessary benchmarks. It is then up to the physician leadership to review these benchmarks on a regular basis, usually monthly, to identify potential problem areas and quickly respond accordingly.

Chapter 2

The Private Insurance System

Before examining how health insurance works in the United States, it is worth considering who does and does not have insurance coverage. According to U.S. Census Bureau figures issued in August 2005, nearly 85 percent of the U.S. population have health insurance.[1] Nearly 60 percent obtain health insurance either through group plans offered by their employers, or as individuals who purchase their own insurance. Federal, state, and local government agencies provide health insurance to an additional 25 percent of the U.S. population.[2] (See Table 2.1 for U.S. health statistics, 1990–2004.) About 15.9 percent, or 46.6 million individuals, were without health insurance (some by choice) at some time during 2005—a record number, which included 8.3 million children.

Health insurance is similar to other insurances in that the insurer pays the medical cost of the insured for a covered illness or accident. The main difference between life and health insurance is that unlike life insurance, health policies generally are in effect for one year, are not guaranteed renewable at the end of that period, and premiums and coverage may change at renewal time. The rising cost of health care premiums has been of great concern to employers and employees alike.

PricewaterhouseCoopers estimates that of the 8.7 percent overall increase in premiums that occurred between 2004 and 2005, 43 percent was due to increased utilization of services, 30 percent to price increases in excess of inflation, and 27 percent was due to general inflation.[3] Increasing utilization seems to be caused by a combination of factors including: increased consumer demand, new medical technology, increased diagnostic testing (probably due to "defensive" medicine), unhealthy lifestyles, and an aging population. In a study of records going back to the 1960s, an MIT professor has concluded that much of the growth in medical spending is due to expansion in availability of insurance and not because of advances in technology.[4]

Table 2.1   National U.S. Health Statistics, 1990–2004

	1990	2000	2004
Gross domestic product (GDP) ($B)	5,803	9,817	11,734
National health expenditures ($B)	717.3	1,385.5	1,887.6
Health expenditures as % of GDP (%)	12.4	13.8	16
Amount per capita ($)	2,821	4,729	6,280
Source of dollars for health care			
Private (%)	59.6	55.7	54.9
Public (%)	40.4	44.3	45.1
Federal (%)	27	30.8	32
State and local (%)	13.4	13.5	13.2
Personal expenditures for health care			
Total ($B)	607.5	1,139.9	1,560.2
Out-of-pocket ($B)	137.8	192.6	235.7
Third-party ($B)			
Private insurance ($B)	203.2	402.7	563.5
Other private funds ($B)	30.6	56.8	68.6
Public funds			
Federal ($B)	174	371.1	529.2
State and local ($B)	63.8	116.6	163.2
Where health care money was spent			
National health expenditures ($B)	717.3	1,385.5	1,887.6
Health care services and supplies ($B)	666.7	1,264.5	1,753
Personal health care ($B)	607.5	1,139.9	1,560.2
Hospital care ($B)	251.6	417	570.8
Physician and clinical services ($B)	157.5	288.6	399.9
Prescription drugs (B$)	40.3	120.8	188.5
Government administration and net cost of private health insurance ($B)	39.2	81.2	136.7

(Table continued on next page)

Table 2.1   National U.S. Health Statistics, 1990–2004 (continued)

	1990	2000	2004
Insurance			
Total with public health insurance ($B)	32.2	35.8	44.6
Medicare ($B)	3.5	5.4	6.3
Medicaid ($B)	22.7	26.2	34.2
Tricare/Champus ($B)	7.9	6.8	7.3
Total with private insurance ($B)	164.7	179.9	176.5
Employer coverage ($B)	149.6	163.8	159.1
Other ($B)	15.1	16.1	17.4
Number of health maintenance organizations (HMOs)	572	568	412
HMO enrollment (millions)	33	80.9	68.8
Hospitals			
Number of hospitals	6,649	5,810	5,759
Number of community hospitals	5,384	4,915	4,919
Number of beds (community hospitals)	927	824	808
Total net margin (%), community hospitals		4.6	5.2
Net patient margin (%), community hospitals		−4.2	−2.3
Physicians			
Number (thousands)	615	814	885
Nurses			
Number, active, registered (thousands)	1,790	2,202	2,394

Sources: "By the Numbers," Supplement, *Modern Healthcare*, 35 (Dec. 19, 2005): 2–40.

Centers for Medicare & Medicaid Services and Office of the Assistant Secretary for Planning and Evaluation, "An Overview of the U.S. Health Care System Chart Book," (Jan. 31, 2007), www.cms.hhs.gov/TheChartSeries/downloads/Chartbook_2007_pdf.pdf (accessed March 7, 2007).

Centers for Medicare & Medicaid Services, Office of the Actuary, National Health Statistics Group, "The Nation's Health Dollar, Calendar Year 2005: Where It Went," www.cms.hhs.gov/NationalHealthExpendData/downloads/PieChartSourcesExpenditures2005 (accessed March 7, 2007).

Centers for Medicare & Medicaid Services, "National Health Expenditures Aggregate, Per Capita Amounts, Percent Distribution, and Average Annual Percent Growth, by Source of Funds: Selected Calendar Years 1960-2005," www.cms.hhs.gov/NationalHealthExpendData/downloads/tables.pdf (accessed March 7, 1007).

Figure 2.1   The Health Care Premium Dollar

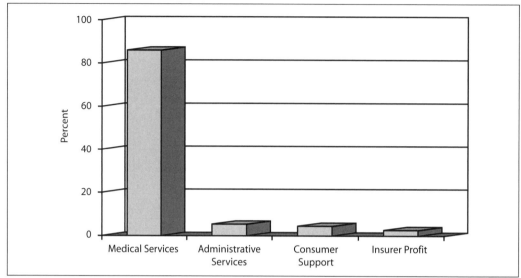

Source: The Factors Fueling Rising Healthcare Costs 2006, prepared for America's Health Insurance Plans, January 2006, PricewaterhouseCoopers. Used with permission.

As indicated in Figure 2.1, the majority of each premium dollar (87 cents) goes to medical services. Components of these services include:

- Physician services, 24 percent;

- Outpatient costs, 22 percent;

- Inpatient costs, 18 percent;

- Prescription costs, 16 percent; and

- Other medical services such as durable medical equipment, 6 percent.

It is estimated that 10 cents of each dollar spent on medical services goes to defensive medicine and related costs of the medical malpractice tort system, while 8.5 percent of the cost of premiums is attributable to providing unreimbursed care to the uninsured.[5] An additional component of medical cost is the expense of the current system of health coverage. A key term to remember in measuring this cost is *medical loss ratio*. The ratio refers to the cost of delivering patient care versus the money collected by the insurance company. The lower the ratio, the fewer dollars are being spent on medical care vs. administrative costs and profits.

Traditional (Fee-for-Service) Insurance

Fee-for-service insurance, sometimes called *traditional insurance*, covers illnesses and injuries. Patients typically owe a copayment or deductible; service providers must send claims to the patient's insurance company to obtain the remainder of their reimbursement. Fee-for-service plans give patients a broad choice of physicians and hospitals in their area, but at the cost of paying a higher premium than for other types of coverage. There are two types of fee-for-service coverage: basic coverage and major medical (see Table 2.2). Basic coverage pays for a hospital stay, some physician fees, limited drug costs, and supplies. Major medical coverage takes over for long-term care and complicated illnesses. A comprehensive insurance policy will offer both types of coverage.

Common features of fee-for-service insurance plans are:

- The insurance company charges the policyholder a monthly fee or premium;

Table 2.2   Types of Insurance

Major Medical Coverage	
Major medical	Coverage for majority of hospital and medical bills.
Managed care	Pays for basic medical care and hospital expenses for in-network physicians and facilities.
Hospital–surgical	Covers only expenses directly related to hospitalization.
Short-term care	Covers short-term needs, such as individuals in-between jobs; offers no coverage for pre-existing conditions.
Catastrophic	High-deductible policy with restrictions for individuals in good health or for those who are otherwise uninsurable.
Limited Purpose Coverage	
Accident only	Pays only when you are treated for accidental injury or if an accident causes death.
Hospital indemnity	Coverage for hospitalization only with a fixed per-diem payment.
Long-term care	Pays to take care of you for an extended time in a nursing home or your own home.
Medicare supplement	Pays some medical expenses not paid by Medicare.
Special need/specific disease	A "boutique" policy that pays for a very small portion of selected conditions, such as cancer, not covered by typical major medical policies .
Home health care	Pays for health care in your home.

Adapted from: Ohio Department of Insurance, Shopper's Guide, www.ohioinsurance.gov. (Information on Website subject to change.)

- The policyholder must pay a deductible for services before insurance payments commence. Only expenses covered under a plan count toward the deductible, which is calculated for each person covered under the policy, and are for amounts spent during one year. After the deductible is satisfied, the rest of the health bill may be shared with the insurance company in a predetermined fashion—usually 80 percent paid by the insurer and 20 percent by the subscriber (copayment);

- There is an annual dollar cap (out-of-pocket expense) for the patient, after which the insurer picks up all medical expenses; and

- Typically, preventive care is not included.

Preferred Provider Organizations

Physicians, hospitals, and other providers contract to become part of preferred provider organizations (PPOs) to provide health care at discounted rates in return for expedited payment, and hopes for increased market share. Patients often have a choice of using PPO or non-PPO providers, but patients have financial incentives (such as lower copayments) to use the PPO network.

Point-of-Service Plans

A point-of-servvice (POS) plan is similar to an HMO in that a subscriber can visit a physician within the network and pay a small copayment. But, in addition, out-of-network physicians can be consulted with the payment of a certain percentage of charges after meeting the deductible. As an example, in-network physicians may be seen with the subscriber paying only 10 percent of the cost of services, but out-of-network services may require payment of 30 percent of cost. These plans usually have restrictions such as limited or no coverage for services such as transplants, infertility treatments, or mental health services, if the subscriber goes outside the network.

Health Maintenance Organizations

The HMO is a legal entity to which its members prepay a premium for their health services. The HMO assumes responsibility for the cost of these members' health care services; thus, it is a form of health insurance. Coverage generally involves a group of physicians and hospitals selected by the insurance company. Patients face greater out-of-pocket costs for using services outside the selected panel. The cost is generally less than a fee-for-service plan, and basic preventive care services are covered. Claims for visiting in-network care providers are usually filed directly with the HMO. In contrast to a PPO, an HMO is usually regulated by the state department of insurance. Other features of HMOs:

- Every subscriber is assigned or selects a primary care physician and usually all referrals to specialists are through the "gatekeeper" physician to keep costs down;

- Preventive care is covered; and

- Usually a membership card is sufficient for identification purposes at a hospital and physician offices, and no billing claim forms may be necessary.

A disadvantage of an HMO is that subscribers (patients) face restrictions on the specialists they may visit. Tighter regulations regarding their coverage when outside the HMO's referral (geographic) area are another disadvantage.

Types of Coverage

Individual. The insured is the policyholder and contracts directly with the company in much the same way as purchasing an auto or home insurance policy. Premium rates can be increased after approval from the state's department of insurance, and affect everyone who has a similar policy. State requirements also may mandate specific minimum benefits and a non-cancellable feature, if the subscriber's health status changes—unless the company can prove the subscriber committed fraud when applying for coverage or failed to pay the premium.

Group. An employer—the master policyholder—purchases a group coverage policy or policies; its employees are the policy's certificate holders. The contract is negotiated by the employer, which has the option to change coverage, premiums, benefits, and insurance companies. The rates are not subject to state regulations and are negotiated by the employer, although states may mandate minimum benefits. Large groups are generally considered to be those of more than 50 employees and, depending on their size, may have enough clout to negotiate more generous benefits at lower rates.

Deductibles, Copayments, and Out-of-Pocket Expenses

Most insurance policies require payment of copayments and deductibles in addition to the monthly premium. Services and costs not covered (such as cosmetic surgery) by the policy do not satisfy deductibles, or out-of-pocket maximums.

Deductible. A set amount is the amount that a subscriber must pay toward covered expenses before the policy starts to pay. Some policies require a payment of a deductible for each incident.

Copayment. The amount is set by the insurance company to represent a subscriber's share of his/her health care expenses.

Out-of-Pocket Expense. This is the maximum amount a covered individual or family will pay annually in combined copayments and deductibles for covered services. Once that amount is exceeded in the plan year, the insurance company will typically pay 100 percent of the remaining amount for eligible services up to a lifetime maximum amount.

It is important to note that deductibles and copayments are separate items.

UCR Payments. The usual and customary (UCR) payment is the amount the insurance company believes to be a fair price for medical services; it may be less than the physician's actual bill. The policyholder is responsible for the balance. The insurance company typically pays a percentage of the UCR amount. As an example: If the insurance company pays 80 percent of the UCR, the policyholder is responsible for the remaining 20 percent plus the difference between the physician's actual bill and the UCR. The state of Ohio does not regulate UCR. Every company has its own way of determining the UCR amount for a service.

Flexible Spending Accounts

Companies may offer employees a medical flexible spending account (FSA) as part of their benefits plan. The employee may then set aside money through regular, equal payroll deductions in order to pay copayments, items that insurance does not cover, and sometimes over-the-counter medicines. FSAs generally do not cover cosmetic services but will cover things such as vision care. The deductions are made before taxes are computed, thus reducing the employee's salary for income-tax purposes. Some companies may also offer a dependent care plan to cover child care or care of a dependent person at home.

A major concern was the "use-it or lose-it" rule with an FSA where all contributions had to be spent by the end of the plan year or else be forfeited. However, the IRS recently loosened the use-it-or-lose-it rule by announcing that it will allow FSA participants to make claims against their accounts for up to 2 months and 15 days after the end of their benefit year. For employees on a calendar benefit year, FSA contributions can now be used for expenses incurred as late as March 15, provided the employer has amended its FSA benefit plan to allow use of this extension period. The IRS also allows use of funds pledged but not yet paid into the account, if emergency out-of-pocket expenses are incurred.

Certain expenses not paid by insurance or other plans may be considered qualified medical expenses under an FSA plan. These expenses include treatment for alcoholism or drug dependency, ambulance services, artificial limbs, artificial teeth, child-care or day-care expenses necessary for employment, chiropractors, and many other services, including medical and prescription coinsurance amounts. A complete list of eligible expenses can be found in IRS Publication 502, accessible through the IRS Website at www.irs.gov. In 2003, the IRS ruled that over-the-counter drugs can be paid for with FSA money.

Health Savings Accounts

Health savings accounts (HSAs)[6] were created by the Medicare Modernization Act of 2003, and are designed to help individuals save for future qualified medical and retiree health expenses on a tax-free basis. HSA accounts are owned by individuals who can make contributions to pay for current and future medical expenses. HSAs are designed to be used in conjunction with high-deductible health plans (HDHPs). A qualifying HDHP plan may be an HMO, PPO, or indemnity plan.

What Is an HDHP?

An HDHP is a health insurance plan with a minimum deductible of:

- $1,050 for self-only coverage or $2,100 for family coverage (2006 amounts);
- Deductibles indexed annually for inflation; and
- Annual out-of-pocket expenses (including deductibles and copays) capped at $5,250 for self-only coverage and $10,500 for family coverage (2006 amounts).

HDHPs may offer first-dollar coverage (no deductible) for preventive care (but with a copayment allowed), and a higher out-of-pocket amount (copayments and coinsurance) for non-network services. The plans also require that all covered benefits, including prescription drug expenses, must be applied to meeting the plan's annual deductible.

Who Is Eligible to Establish an HSA?

Any individual may establish an HSA who:

- Is covered by an HDHP;
- Is not covered by other health insurance;
- Is not enrolled in Medicare; and
- Cannot be claimed as a dependent on someone else's tax return.

Additional HSA rules to remember are that:

- Children cannot establish their own HSAs;
- Spouses can establish their own HSAs, if eligible;

- There are no income limits on whom may contribute to an HSA; and

- There is no requirement to have an earned income to contribute to an HSA.

What Are the Important HSA Contribution Rules?

An individual, the individual's employer, or both may make contributions to HSAs under the following rules:

- Contributions made by the employer are not taxable to the employee (that is, they are excluded from the individual's income and wages);

- Contributions made by individuals are considered "above-the-line" deductions; and

- Contributions can be made by others on behalf of the individual and deducted by the individual.

The maximum amount that can be contributed to (and deducted from) an HSA from all sources is the lesser of the HDHP deductible amount, or the maximum specified by law for the current year ($2,700 for individual coverage and $5,450 for family coverage in 2006).

How Does an Individual's Age Affect HSA Contributions?

For individuals age 55 and older, additional catch-up contributions may be made to an HSA in the following amounts: $700 for 2006, $800 for 2007, $900 for 2008, and $1,000 for 2009 and after. The contributions must stop once an individual is enrolled in Medicare. Contributions made to the HSA in excess of contribution limits must be withdrawn by the individual or be subject to an excise tax.

How Are Contributions Made to an HSA?

Employee contributions to an HSA can be made by a salary-reduction arrangement through a cafeteria plan (Section 125 plan). Elections to make contributions through a cafeteria plan can change on a month-by-month basis (unlike salary-reduction contributions to an FSA. Contributions to the HSA through a cafeteria plan are considered pre-tax, and therefore not subject to individual or employment taxes. Employers can automatically make FSA contributions on an individual's behalf, unless the individual affirmatively elects not to have such contributions made (negative elections).

Employer contributions to an HSA are always excluded from the employee's income (pre-tax). Contributions must be comparable for all employees participating in the HSA. Contributions not comparable are subject to an excise tax equal to 35 percent of the amount the employer contributed to employees' HSAs. The self-employed, partner–owners, and S corporation shareholders are generally not considered employees and cannot receive an employer contribution. They can make deductible contributions to the HSA on their own.

How Are Funds Distributed from an HSA?

Distributions are tax-free if taken for qualified medical expenses. A qualified medical expense must be incurred on or after the date the HSA was established. Therefore, if HDHP coverage is effective on the first day of month, an HSA can be established as early as the first day of the same month. If HDHP coverage becomes effective on any day other than first day of month, the HSA cannot be established until the first day of the following month.

COBRA Insurance Coverage

The Consolidated Omnibus Budget Reconciliation Act of 1985 (COBRA)[7] mandates that employers must permit certain employees to continue health insurance coverage after they leave employment.

When Are You Entitled to COBRA Coverage?

- Your group health plan must be covered by COBRA;
- A qualifying event must occur; and
- You must be a qualified beneficiary for that event.

What Is the Cost of COBRA Coverage?

The employer is not required to pay for the continuation of health insurance coverage, but must allow the employee to purchase coverage for no more than 102 percent of the premium the employer previously paid. The employer can add a 2-percent administrative cost to the premium. The employee may also be able to purchase lesser types of coverage, if the employer has already offered that coverage to employees. Although the employee is not required to send in an initial payment with the election form choosing COBRA, the initial premium payment must be made within 45 days after the date of COBRA election. Failure to make any payment within the 45 days can cause the loss of all COBRA rights. The plan can set premium due dates for successive periods of coverage (after the initial payment), but it must give the individual the option to make monthly payments, and it must allow a 30-day grace period for payment of any premium.

Whom Is the Coverage Offered To?

COBRA requires continuation coverage to be offered to covered employees, their spouses, their former spouses, and their dependent children when group health coverage would otherwise be lost due to certain specific events.

When Is COBRA Coverage Available?

Those events include the death of a covered employee, termination or reduction in the hours of a covered employee's employment for reasons other than gross misconduct, and divorce or legal separation from a covered employee. A covered employee's spouse is eligible for COBRA if the employee becomes entitled to Medicare (and therefore is not covered by the company's health plan).

Which Employers Are Required to Offer COBRA?

COBRA generally applies to all group health plans maintained by private-sector employers (with at least 20 employees), or by state and local governments.

How Long Is COBRA Coverage Required?

COBRA requires that continuation coverage be made available for a limited period of time, either 18 or 36 months. There is nothing in law that prevents an employer from providing coverage longer than COBRA requirements. The duration of coverage depends upon the type of event that led to COBRA coverage. If termination of employment or reduction in employment hours was the event, employees may be entitled to a maximum of 18 months of coverage. If a similar event occurred for a person who became entitled to Medicare less than 18 months before the qualifying event, COBRA coverage may be required for 36 months. The usual 18-month period may be extended if the employee or a qualified family member becomes disabled, or when a second qualifying event occurs. Another circumstance where the period of coverage is extended to 29 months is when a qualified family member becomes disabled. In this scenario, the employer is allowed to charge up to 150 percent of the cost of usual coverage for 11 months of additional coverage.

Other Federal Laws Related to Health Insurance Coverage

The Family and Medical Leave Act (FMLA) requires employers to maintain coverage under any group health plan for an employee on FMLA leave under the same conditions coverage would have been provided had the employee continued working.

The Health Insurance Portability and Accountability Act also provides special enrollment rights upon the loss of group health plan coverage.

These rights to buy individual coverage do not impose a pre-existing condition exclusion period.

Complaints Against Health Insurance Companies

Each state's department of insurance is responsible for regulating all insurance companies, and tracking and resolving complaints (see Appendix D on the CD for a list of state insurance commissioners). In Ohio, the top 10 reasons for health insurance complaints are: claim denial; claim delay; unsatisfactory settlement offer; coverage questions; premium and rating issues; cancellation; premium refunds; premium notice and billing issues; usual, customary, and reasonable issues; and other issues.[8]

Laws Related to Prompt Payment of Medical Claims

Some states have laws that hold insurance companies responsible for delaying payment, or not being transparent enough in their policy-making. Physician groups in a national class action suit against major insurance companies, including Aetna and CIGNA, alleged unfair business practices. A settlement was reached by most of the insurers named in the action and some of these industry practices have been curtailed by law. The legislature in Ohio, for example, acted to increase transparency by requiring the following:[9]

- Payment rule disclosure: Insurance contracts with physicians must state the rights and responsibilities of the insurer regarding payment policies, administrative policies, utilization policies, and the like;

- Fee schedule disclosure: Insurers must provide a fee schedule;

- Fair payment rules that call for insurers to use the most up-to-date Current Procedural Terminology and International Classification of Diseases, 9th revision, codes;

- Well-woman code that allows women to visit OB/GYN physicians without requiring a referral from a primary care physician; and

- Timely payment rules that call for insurers to pay or deny claims to physicians within 30 days. If additional documentation is needed, insurers have 45 days after receipt of the additional material in which to approve or deny the claim.

Summary

Physicians are not only providers of care but consumers also. A change in employment requires attention to health coverage for themselves and their dependents. In addition, it also falls on most medical offices to be cognizant of the terminology that health plans use in order to better educate their patients.

References

1. U.S. Census Bureau, "Income, Poverty, and Health Insurance Coverage in the United States: 2005," issued August 2006, www.census.gov/prod/2006pubs/p60-231.pdf (accessed Sept. 5, 2006).

2. The Commonwealth Fund, "Number of Uninsured Americans Increases in 2004," *Washington Health Policy Week in Review,* (Sept. 6, 2005) www.cmwf.org/healthpolicyweek/healthpolicyweek_show.htm?doc_id=295101 (accessed April 23, 2007).

3. PricewaterhouseCoopers, "The Factors Fueling Rising Healthcare Costs 2006," prepared for America's Health Insurance Plans, (January 2006) www.pwc.com/us/eng/about/ind/healthcare/pubfuel.html (accessed Aug. 3, 2006).

4. H. Gleckman, "So That's Why It's So Expensive," *Business Week Online,* Aug. 14, 2006, www.businessweek.com/magazine/toc/06_33/B3997magazine.htm (accessed Aug. 5, 2006).

5. Families USA, "Paying a Premium: The Added Cost of Care for the Uninsured," June 2005, www.familiesusa.org/assets/pdfs/Paying_a_Premium_rev_July_13731e.pdf (accessed Aug. 6, 2006).

6. U.S. Department of the Treasury, "All About HSAs," Powerpoint presentation, Nov. 28, 2005, www.treasury.gov/offices/public-affairs/hsa/pdf/hsa-basics.pdf (accessed Aug. 4, 2006).

7. U.S. Department of Labor, Employee Benefits Security Administration, "An Employee's Guide to Health Benefits Under COBRA," www.dol.gov/ebsa/pdf/cobraemployee.pdf (accessed Aug. 3, 2006).

8. Ohio Department of Insurance, "Shoppers Guide to Health Insurance and HMOs," www.ohioinsurance.gov/ConsumServ/Ocs/CompleteGuides/HealthComplaints.pdf (accessed Aug. 6, 2006).

9. Ohio State Medical Association, www.osma.org (accessed Aug. 6, 2006).

Chapter 3

How Medicare Works

Medicare is the largest, primary social health insurance program in the United States. It covered more than 42 million Americans and consumed about 3.2 percent of the national gross domestic product (GDP) in 2006. The program was enacted as Title XVIII of the Social Security Act, designated "Health Insurance for the Aged and Disabled" (P.L. 89–97, 89th Congress) on July 30, 1965. It now covers one of every seven Americans at an annual projected cost exceeding $330 billion (2006). Eligible beneficiaries include individuals who are:

- Age 65 or older;
- Disabled and entitled to Social Security benefits or railroad retirement benefits; or
- Enrolled in the End Stage Renal Disease program.

The Centers for Medicare and Medicaid Services (CMS), under the Department of Health and Human Services (HHS), administers the Medicare program. However, an application for Medicare enrollment is done through the Social Security Administration (SSA) by visiting the local SSA office or calling 800.772.1213.

The Four Parts of Medicare

Medicare has four parts, which are discussed in the following sections.

Part A or Hospital Insurance

Medicare Part A is paid primarily through a 2.9-percent payroll tax shared equally between employees and employers. For the self-employed, the Part A withholding tax is 2.9 percent. Most individuals (99 percent) covered by Part A qualified based on the number of quarters they worked, and pay no premiums.

Beneficiaries pay a deductible for inpatient hospital admissions equal to the cost of one hospital day, which was $992 in 2007 (Table 3.1). They also pay hospital coinsurance, which is set at 25 percent of the hospital deductible for admission days 61 through 90. Medicare Part A coverage also can be purchased by those age over age 65, enrolled in Part B, and

Table 3.1   Medicare Premiums and Deductibles, 2007

	Monthly Premium	Annual Deductible
Part A (hospital)	$410 (paid by only 1% of beneficiaries)	$992
Part B (SMI)	$93.50	$131
Part D (drug benefit)	$27.35	$265

Source: Centers for Medicare and Medicaid Services (Sept. 12, 2006), "Medicare Premiums and Deductibles for 2007," www.cms.hhs.gov/apps/media/press/release.asp?Counter=1958 (accessed April 23, 2007).

Table 3.2   Medicare Funding Sources

Source	Part A	Part B	Part D
General tax revenues		✓	✓
Premiums from beneficiaries		✓	✓
Payroll taxes	✓		
Interest on government securities	✓	✓	✓

Source: Centers for Medicare and Medicaid Services (May 1, 2006), "2006 Medicare Trustees Report," www.cms.hhs.gov/apps/media/press/release.asp?Counter=1846 (accessed April 23, 2007).

either citizens or legal immigrants living in the U.S for at least five years. The program provides beneficiaries:

- Inpatient hospital care, including 90 days of inpatient stay per benefit period;

- Limited nursing home care—up to 100 post-hospital days in a skilled nursing home facility; and

- Home health services: unlimited visits by a home health nurse.

Part B or Supplemental Medical Insurance

Medicare Part B, or supplemental medical insurance (SMI), is financed by enrollee premiums (25 percent), and by general revenues from the federal treasury and interest earned on the Part B trust fund (75 percent), as shown in Table 3.2. In 2007, beneficiaries paid a $131 annual deductible.

Part B is voluntary, but 97 percent of those who participate in Part A choose to enroll in Part B. Most enrollees paid monthly premiums of $93.50 in 2007. Premiums are based on a sliding scale depending on modified adjusted gross income (a combination of adjusted gross [taxable] income and tax-exempt interest income) supplied by the IRS. Those with income less than 135 percent of federal poverty threshold, which is updated annually by the U.S. Census Bureau, receive subsidies for part or all of their premiums. One-fourth of all beneficiaries receive some sort of assistance for Parts B and D or both.

Part B insurance pays for:

- Physician services in offices, inpatient or outpatient areas, rural health clinics, and ambulatory surgical centers;
- Ambulance transportation;
- Home health services;
- Clinical laboratories and diagnostic services;
- Surgical supplies;
- Durable medical equipment and supplies such as wheelchairs and walking aids; and
- Limited license providers such as advanced registered nurse practitioners, independent physical therapists and occupational therapists, optometrists, midwives, audiologists, licensed social workers, clinical psychologists, physician assistants, and certified registered nurse anesthetists.

Part C: The Medicare Advantage Plan

Part C, which was implemented via the Balanced Budget Act of 1997 (BBA), allows Medicare recipients to participate in Part C type plans, which may include: health maintenance organizations (HMOs), preferred provider organizations (PPOs), point-of-service organizations (POSs), and medical savings accounts. In 2006, approximately 15 percent of beneficiaries were enrolled in these plans.

Part D: The Medicare Prescription Drug Benefit

Created by the Medicare Prescription Drug, Improvement and Modernization Act (MMA) of 2003, Medicare Part D is funded through a separate account within the Part B trust fund, with 25 percent of revenues coming from premiums and the rest from general revenues.

Beneficiaries, in general, are required to pay:

- A monthly premium of $27.35;
- An annual deductible amount of $265; and
- Coinsurance of 25 percent up to a coverage limit of $2,400, including deductibles.

The program provides complete coverage of prescription drug costs over $3,850 per year, but there is a gap in coverage for annual expenses between $2,400 and $3,850. Medicare beneficiaries without prescription benefits are now eligible for prescription drug cards. These cards were made available in 2004 with the full benefit effective in 2006. Low-income Medicare recipients do not pay monthly deductibles or monthly premiums and have no gaps in coverage. They also become eligible for additional financial assistance of $600 annually in addition to the prescription drug coverage. By the time the program initial sign-up period ended on May 15, 2006, more than 30 million beneficiaries had signed up for Part D coverage.

For now, Canadian drug imports are allowed only if HHS considers them safe, but otherwise maintains the ban on drug importation. Additional aspects of the program call for:

- Medicare to contract with private companies to administer the drug benefit;

- Competition for coverage of the drug benefit to be encouraged starting in 2010; and

- All new Medicare entrants to be allowed a free physical screening examination within six months of joining, including diabetes screening and some cardiovascular blood tests.

Medicare Coverage for Immigrants

Immigrants legally in the United States may be eligible for Medicare benefits after they have resided in the country for five consecutive years. At that time, they have the option for entering one or more parts of Medicare. New immigrants who paid Medicare taxes for more than 30, but less than 40 quarters, are eligible to purchase Part A coverage for $216 a month in 2006, and for $393 a month if they have less than 30 quarters.

Questions and Answers About Medicare

What Qualifies as a Medicare Part B Health Professional Shortage Area?

The Census Bureau determines which cities or counties or portions of those areas are deemed health professional shortage areas (HPSAs). These medically underserved areas (which can be rural or urban) are eligible for incentive payments that are generally 10 percent of the amount paid to the physician in the previous quarter. To obtain these payments, physicians in an HPSA should mark the claim form either with modifier QB (physician service in a rural HPSA) or QU (physician service in an urban HPSA).

What Do Medicare Contractors Do?

There are two types of Medicare contractors:

- *Intermediaries* that process Part A (hospital insurance) services such as inpatient hospital admissions, skilled nursing homes, home health agencies, and hospices. Intermediaries (such as Blue Cross and Blue Shield) also determine costs and reimbursement amounts, maintain records, perform reviews and audits to prevent fraud and abuse, make payments to providers, and assist beneficiaries as well as providers; and

- *Carriers,* which can be commercial companies such as Aetna or CIGNA. Carriers handle Part B (SMI) claims for services provided by physicians and medical suppliers. They also determine Medicare-allowed charges, maintain records, make payments to physicians and suppliers, assist in fraud and abuse investigations, and assist beneficiaries and payees.

What Is the Relationship Between Medicare and Medicaid?

Medicaid provides some level of supplemental coverage for about 5 million Medicare beneficiaries. When a person is covered by both programs, providers should seek reimbursement from Medicare as the patient's primary insurance before billing Medicaid as the patient's secondary insurance.

The four categories of Medicare beneficiaries who may also be eligible for Medicaid benefits are:

- Persons who have low income and limited resources. Each state sets eligibility criteria that may cover nursing home care beyond the 100-day limit under Medicare, prescription drugs, eyeglasses, or hearing aids;

- Qualified Medicare beneficiaries who have resources at or below 100 percent of the federal poverty threshold. Medicaid will pay these individuals' Medicare Part A and Part B premiums, coinsurance, and deductibles within state guidelines and limits;

- Specified low-income beneficiaries. These individuals are also Medicare beneficiaries with limited financial resources, with incomes less than 120 percent of the federal poverty threshold. Medicaid will only pay for the Part B premiums of these individuals; and

- Disabled and working individuals who previously qualified for Medicare due to disability, but lost entitlement because they returned to work despite their disability. Those eligible are allowed by law to purchase Part A and Part B coverage.

How Do Physicians Enroll for Medicare Part B?

Enroll. Physicians are required to complete Form CMS-855 (provider/supplier enrollment application). The completed application is sent to the local carrier's provider enrollment department. To find a list of local carriers, see the CMS Webpage, www.cms.hhs.gov/providers/enrollment. Individual physicians should complete and submit Form CMS-855I; medical groups and clinics should complete and submit Form CMS-855B. In addition, medical groups and clinics must fill out Form CMS-855R, which reassigns all payments for individual physicians to the group or clinic entity.

Obtain a PIN. The carrier then processes the application and provides an personal identification number (PIN), which is used for billing and all communications with the carrier. If a bill is sent to a carrier without a PIN, it will be returned as "unprocessable."

Obtain a UPIN, if needed. This six-digit unique physician identification number (UPIN) is used only when a service requires an ordering or referring physician, not for billing purposes. It is required for services such as consultations, routine foot care, durable medical equipment, orthotics, prosthetics, radiology, and laboratory diagnostic services. This number is portable from state to state. Surrogate UPINs are assigned for interns, residents, and fellows (RES000).

Obtain an NPI. The Health Insurance Portability and Accountability Act of 1996 (HIPAA) called for four identification numbers, including a national provider identifier (NPI) number. This 10-digit, numeric identifier will stay constant for each physician or other health care entity and will be used by CMS for all transactions. The NPI number must have been obtained by May 23, 2007. As of April 2006, HHS reports that roughly 20 percent of the 2 million expected applicants had NPI numbers assigned. HHS also estimates that net savings from reducing costs and gaining efficiency to all health plans and providers by instituting a national identifier will amount to $426 million between 2007–2011. CMS has already started processing provider applications in batches or *bulk enumeration*.[1] A paper application form can be obtained by calling 800.465.3203 or online at the CMS Webpage, https://NPPES.cms.hhs.gov.

Are Fewer Physicians Accepting Medicare Each Year?

Because Medicare reimbursement to physicians has been decreased on a regular basis by Congress, the concern has been that physicians would stop accepting new patients with Medicare. The Center for Studying Health System Change released a community tracking study of patient access to physicians. The data, which used a sample of physicians from the master files of the American Medical Association (AMA) and the American Osteopathic Association, suggests that about 73 percent of physicians are accepting all new Medicare patients, and that this rate stabilized in 2005 from 1996–1997.[2] Other findings of the survey showed:

- The proportion of primary care physicians accepting Medicare increased from 61.7 percent to 65.3 percent in 2004–2005, whereas the specialist's participation remained the same. This is likely because primary care physicians generally earn less than the specialists, and because of the decrease in reimbursement from private carriers. Medicare patients have become a major source of revenue;

- Only 3.4 percent of physicians accepted no new Medicare patients. Two-thirds of these physicians cited low reimbursement, billing and paperwork, higher clinical burden associated with older patients, an already busy practice, and fear of an audit as the reasons for declining new Medicare patients; and

- Even though office visits by Medicare-eligible patients have stabilized to about 5.5 physician visits a year per patient, the overall growth of volume and intensity of services—mostly the number of tests and procedures—have increased, leading to payment cuts to meet budgetary constraints.

What Is the Basis for Reimbursement for Medicare?

There are two common methods to reimburse physicians for their services. The fee-schedule method is typically used when the physician has contracted to accept a fee schedule for various services, such as under the resource-based relative value scale (RBRVS) discussed later. The second method is payment based upon a negotiated percentage of charges set by the physician. Hospitals, on the other hand, may be paid per case (inpatient payment under the diagnosis-related group [DRG] system for Medicare), per diem (a common method several years ago and used currently by some HMOs), or as a percentage of charges (negotiated with some private insurers).

Which Government Agency Recommends Changes in the Reimbursement to Physicians?

The Medicare Payment Advisory Commission (MedPAC), the independent group appointed by Congress as part of the BBA, is charged with reviewing Medicare payment policies, and recommending changes to cover the cost of the Medicare program.[3]

How Do Physicians Get Reimbursed Under Medicare?

Medicare pays physicians based on a fee schedule that assigns each service relative weights. Although Medicare payment rates have been traditionally lower then private insurers, the gap has narrowed between 1994–2004. Averaged across all services and areas, 2004 Medicare rates were 83 percent of private insurance rates (up from 66 percent in the mid-1990s). Looking at it another way, Medicare average fees for physician services grew about 2 percent in 2004 compared to 1 percent for private insurance payments. Medicaid fees are even lower, currently at 69 percent of Medicare fees (2003); they have increased from 64 percent of Medicare fees in 1998.[2] Under Medicare Part B, with some exceptions, when there is 100 percent reimbursement, physicians are reimbursed at 80 percent of the lower of the established fee schedule, reasonable or customary charge, or the billed charge. Payment limits also exist for services performed in facilities such as ambulatory surgery centers.

What Are the Options for Getting Reimbursed by Medicare?

Each year from mid-November to December 31, Medicare allows physicians one opportunity to change their participation status for the following calendar year starting January 1. After the participation status is submitted, the physician is contractually bound to it for one year unless he/she moves to a different location, or changes from one group to another. If the physician chooses to change this status, Form CMS 460 needs to be filled out and returned to Medicare. If there is no change in status, no action is required. A physician has three choices when deciding whether to treat patients covered by the Medicare program: participating, non-participating, or opting out of the Medicare program entirely.

Participating in Medicare and Other Options

Participating, frequently shortened to *par*, identifies a physician who enters into an agreement with Medicare to accept payment for all services performed (called *assignment*) on Medicare beneficiaries based on the Medicare-approved amount (according to the Medicare fee schedule). This is 80 percent of the approved amount, plus a 20-percent copayment from the patient or secondary insurance. Balance billing, charging the patient for the difference between the amount billed and the Medicare approved amount, is not allowed. As an incentive to participate, Medicare allows 5 percent higher fee schedules for participating physicians; it does not set limits on their actual charges. In addition, Medicare publishes a list of participating physicians and provides it to the program's beneficiaries. It also makes available toll-free phone numbers to help those physician offices speed up the adjudication of claim payments.

Non-participating

The term *non-participating*, or *non-par*, means the physician can make the decision to accept assignment on a case-by-case basis. When physicians accept the assigned Medicare payment, they accept the Medicare-approved amount at 95 percent of the rate for a participating physician. Non-par physicians can also accept Medicare on a case-by-case assignment. They can charge more than the Medicare-approved amount, but not in excess of 115 percent of the approved Medicare rates for participating physicians.

Opting Out

A third option is to not sign any contract with Medicare and bill patients directly for services. Once physicians elect this option, they sign an affidavit with specific language mandated by Medicare. In addition, patients must also sign a contract agreeing to the terms and conditions. The physician cannot submit any claims to Medicare for two years after choosing this option.

What Is the Limiting Charge?

A *limiting charge* is the maximum amount that a non-participating physician may legally charge any Medicare beneficiary for any services billed on an unassigned claim. These limits are not applicable to participating physicians, or to a non-participating physician who later bills Medicare on an assigned basis. Limiting charge rules do not apply to services not covered under Medicare (for example, cosmetic procedures).

What is "Accepting Assignment?"

For both participating and non-participating physicians, assignment implies that Medicare pays the physician 80 percent of the approved fees (see Table 3.3). In this example, Medicare's approved fee was $100, of which $80, or 80 percent, was paid directly to the physician. Participating physicians receive payment directly from Medicare, whereas payments for services provided by non-participating physicians are mailed to those physicians' patients.

Using the same example for a non-participating physician who does not agree to accept assignment, Medicare allows the physician to collect a

Table 3.3   Participating vs. Non-participating Physician

Participating Physician Who Must Always Accept Assignment:	
Charge submitted to Medicare	$125
Medicare allowed fee	$100
Payment to physician	$80 (80% of allowed fee)
Physician bills patient	$20 (20% coinsurance of $100)
Non-participating Physician Does Not Accept Assignment:	
Charge submitted to Medicare	$109.25 (limiting charge)
Medicare allowed fee	$95 (non-participating fee schedule)
Patient paid by Medicare	$76 (80% of fee schedule), patient pays physician
Physician bills patient	$33.25 (difference between limiting charge $109.25 and 80% of fee schedule $76, which includes a copayment of $19 and a further payment of $14.25)

Source: U.S. Congress, Congressional Budget Office, "Physician Payment Reform Under Medicare," CBO Publication 515 (April 1990), 4.

maximum of $109.25 (95 percent of $100 times 115 percent) and sends $76 to the patient. The physician is then responsible for collecting the $76 plus a copayment of $19 and the additional $14.25 for a total of $109.25.

If a physician accepts assignment (as most do), the Medicare beneficiary is responsible for:

Applicable coinsurance amounts. Coinsurance is generally 20 percent of the Medicare fee schedule and is the amount Medicare will not pay. This amount is paid either by the beneficiary or the supplemental insurance company. The 20 percent amount must be collected from the patient. An effort to routinely waive this collection may be viewed as program abuse. If the patient is unable to pay this amount, a waiver explaining the financial hardship must be obtained, or documentation must be made of a "normal and reasonable" attempt to collect this amount.

Unmet deductibles. Medicare has deductible amounts for both Parts A and B that have to be collected before it makes payment for any services. The same precautions for collection apply to coinsurance amounts.

Excluded services. Medicare excludes certain services, such as non-reconstructive cosmetic surgery, experimental procedures, and most routine physical checkups.

Deciding Whether to Participate in Medicare

The decision whether to be a participating or non-participating physician depends on many factors. An analysis must be made of the volume of Medicare patients in the practice (a high percentage for vascular diseases vs. a low percentage for sports medicine), and whether the collection rate will be better by being a participating physician. Non-participating physicians would need to collect the full limiting charge amount roughly 35 percent of the time they provide a given service in order for the revenues from the service to equal those of participating physicians for the same service.[4]

Using the Advance Beneficiary Notice

The patient should be asked to sign the Advance Beneficiary Notice (ABN), shown in Figure 3.1, when Medicare is not expected to pay for a service judged "not medically necessary" or not "reasonable" that is provided by the physician.[5] A claim is still required to be filed with Medicare for a covered service with a modifier indicating that the office has a signed waiver on file. Two common situations necessitating an ABN are:

- a diagnosis code is unlisted when performing a procedure; and
- a service is performed more frequently than listed (example: screening mammograms).

An ABN is not necessary when the service is non-covered, such as a cosmetic procedure, although if it is not clear and the patient may decide to submit a claim later, the waiver may be needed. The notice must inform the patient why Medicare may deny the service and must be signed prior to the service. While a blanket waiver is not acceptable, a standard waiver on the practice stationery and letterhead with specific procedure filled in is acceptable.

Filing Claims Under Medicare

Physicians cannot charge Medicare patients for either completing or filing a claim for services. Claims may be filed with the Part B carrier either electronically by the physician's office/billing service, or by paper claim (Form CMS-1500) when a paper claim is not prohibited under Medicare mandatory filing requirements effective Oct. 16, 2003, and later. Medicare carriers usually pay "clean" electronic claims by electronic data interchange (EDI) on the 14th day after submission and paper claims after 27 days. Advantages of EDI filing are direct electronic fund transfer to the physician's financial institution, and being able to obtain a status report on pending claims and determine eligibility, as well as whether patients have met their Medicare deductible.

Figure 3.1   Advance Beneficiary Notice

Patient's Name:	Medicare # (HICN):

Advance Beneficiary Notice (ABN)

NOTE: You need to make a choice about receiving these health care items or services.

We expect that Medicare will not pay for the item(s) or service(s) that are described below. Medicare does not pay for all of your health care costs. Medicare only pays for covered items and services when Medicare rules are met. The fact that Medicare may not pay for a particular item or service does not mean that you should not receive it. There may be a good reason your doctor recommended it. Right now, in your case, **Medicare probably will not pay for:**

Items or Services:	
Because:	

The purpose of this form is to help you make an informed choice about whether or not you want to receive these items or services, knowing that you might have to pay for them yourself. Before you make a decision about your options, you should **read this entire notice carefully.**

- Ask us to explain, if you don't understand why Medicare probably won't pay.
- Ask us how much these items or services will cost you (**Estimated Cost:** $_____), in case you have to pay for them yourself or through other insurance.

PLEASE CHOOSE **ONE** OPTION. CHECK **ONE** BOX. **SIGN AND DATE** YOUR CHOICE.

☐ **Option 1. YES. I want to receive these items or services.**

I understand that Medicare will not decide whether to pay unless I receive these items or services. Please submit my claim to Medicare. I understand that you may bill me for items or services and that I may have to pay the bill while Medicare is making its decision. If Medicare does pay, you will refund to me any payments I made to you that are due to me. If Medicare denies payment, I agree to be personally and fully responsible for payment. That is, I will pay personally, either out of pocket or through any other insurance that I have. I understand I can appeal Medicare's decision.

☐ **Option 2. NO. I have decided not to receive these items or services.**

I will not receive these items or services. I understand that you will not be able to submit a claim to Medicare and that I will not be able to appeal your opinion that Medicare won't pay.

_____   _____
Date   Signature of patient or person acting on patient's behalf

NOTE: **Your health information will be kept confidential.** Any information that we collect about you on this form will be kept confidential in our offices. If a claim is submitted to Medicare, your health information on this form may be shared with Medicare. Your health information which Medicare sees will be kept confidential by Medicare.

OMB Approval No. 0938-0566   Form No. CMS-R-131-G   (June 2002)

How Physicians Have Fared Under Medicare

Reimbursement for physician services started with "reasonable and customary" fees. A major change was the RBRVS in 1992.[6] This called for a payment system similar to the DRG method for reimbursing hospitals. Visits to primary care physicians were favorably reimbursed, whereas specialty physicians had major reductions in their fee schedules. The BBA of 1997 cut approximately $11.7 billion over 5 years from physician fees. Under the MMA of 2003, physicians received a 1.5 percent increase in 2004 and a further increase of 1.5 percent planned in 2005—instead of a previously mandated 4.5 percent decrease in reimbursement. CMS recently proposed cuts in physician reimbursements by almost 26 percent (5 percent each year) by 2011, starting with a 4.3 percent cut on Jan. 1, 2006.

As an illustration of the inability to keep up with inflation, physician practice expenses have increased by 40 percent in the past decade, but Medicare reimbursements have increased by only 19 percent during the same period.[7] Payments to physicians vary based on a formula that takes into account a sustainable growth rate (SGR), and a set of projections made by trustees of Medicare and Social Security. CMS announced that physician reimbursement was set to be cut by 4.6 percent in 2007 because spending on physician services increased by 8.5 percent in 2005, with 7.5 percent of the growth ascribed to the volume and intensity of service. This cut, which was again averted by Congress, was based on what several physician organizations believe is faulty SGR methodology.

An AMA survey estimated that based on projected pay cuts of 34 percent and increases in practice costs of 22 percent over the next 9 years, 73 percent of physicians will defer purchase of new equipment and two-thirds will postpone buying any new information technology.[8] CMS has stated that in general, growth in evaluation and management codes accounts for the largest part of growth in physician services. Other areas where growth in physician spending has occurred are: imaging (16 percent), laboratory and other tests (11 percent), and procedures (9 percent).

The Sustainable Growth Rate

Prior to 1989, Medicare payments to physicians grew at an unsustainable 14 percent average annual rate.[9] To curtail growth in spending, Congress linked physician payment to the resources used to provide care. In 1997, Congress came up with a formula (SGR) that set a target rate of growth in spending on physician services and tied it to the national economy. The formula is based upon the estimate of the change in each of four factors:[10]

1. The estimated percentage change in fees for physicians' services;

2. The estimated change in the average number of Medicare fee-for-service beneficiaries;

3. The estimated 10-year average annual growth in real GDP per capita; and

4. The estimated change in expenditures due to changes in law or regulations.

The Impact of the SGR Formula on Physician Fees

Organized medicine has argued that the SGR has several inherent flaws:

- Drug costs have been incorrectly included in the formula;

- Use of the GDP as a standard;

- No provision for new technologies or services; and

- Use of temporary patches to compensate for inherent problems with the SGR, which exacerbates the duration of the cuts.

Since 2002, Congress has used a "band-aid" approach by annually reversing the mandated annual cuts in physician payments without altering the SGR. Medical professional organizations have strongly recommended that Congress link payments to actual practice expenses and delete supplies and services "incident to" physician services, such as prescription drug costs from the SGR. With budgetary pressures, these alterations in the SGR seem like an unlikely scenario as CMS estimates this will cost the U.S. Treasury between $183 billion and $215 billion in additional outlays. If the SGR formula is not altered, physician reimbursement will be cut by more than 30 percent from 2006 to 2012.

Outlook for 2007 and Beyond

According to CMS, the Medicare Economic Index indicates input prices for physician services will increase by 3.7 percent in 2007 and the MedPAC goal for productivity growth in 2007 is 0.9 percent. This would increase federal spending in the program by less than $1.5 billion in the first year and $5 billion to $10 billion over 5 years. But, under the SGR there would have to be reductions in payment from 2007 to 2011 to keep the annual updates budget neutral. MedPAC has recommended to Congress that the substantial negative updates from 2007 to 2011 be cancelled and payments be updated by the projected change in input prices (3.7 percent), less MedPAC's expectation for productivity growth (0.9 percent).

Congressional Committees that Deal with Medicare

The U.S. House of Representatives' committees that consider Medicare issues are the Ways and Means Committee, the Appropriations Committee, and the Energy and Commerce Committee. In the Senate, the Appropriations Committee, the Finance Committee, and the Energy and Commerce Committee address matters dealing with Medicare.

Summary

Medicare has provided much needed health care for the elderly and represents a significant portion of practice revenue for physicians. A general understanding of the Medicare program, reimbursement policies, and the economic basis for future fee updates are essential for most medical practices.

References

1. J. Conn, "Doing a Number on Providers," *Modern Healthcare*, 36 (25) (2006): 50–51.

2. P. Cunningham, A. Staiti, and P. Ginsburg, "Physician Acceptance of New Medicare Patients Stabilizes in 2004–2005," Center for Studying Health System Change, Tracking Report No. 12 (January 2006) www.hschange.com/CONTENT/811/?words=Medicare+patients (accessed May 16, 2006).

3. Medicare Payment Advisory Committee, www.medpac.gov.

4. American Medical Association, "Medicare Participation Options for Physicians," Medicare Physician Payment Action Kit, November 2006, www.ama-assn.org/ama1/pub/upload/mm/-1/medicareoptions.pdf (accessed May 20, 2006).

5. Centers for Medicare and Medicaid Services, "Advance Beneficiary Notice (ABN)," www.cms.hhs.gov/BNI/Downloads/CMSR131G.pdf (accessed May 16, 2006).

6. W.C. Hsiao, and others. *A National Study of Resource-Based Relative Value Scales for Physicians' Services: Final Report* (Cambridge, Mass.: Department of Health Policy and Management, Harvard School of Public Health, and Department of Psychology, Harvard University, 1988), (Supplemental Report and Phase II Final Report).

7. S. Turney, Testimony to U.S. Congress, House Committee on Energy and Commerce, Subcommittee on Health, Feb. 14, 2002, "Medicare Payment Policy: Ensuring Stability and Access Through Physician Payments," 107th Cong., 2nd session, http://energycommerce.house.gov/reparchives/107/hearings/02142002Hearing488/Turney831.htm (accessed April 25, 2007).

8. American Medical Association, (March 16, 2006), "New AMA Survey Shows Medicare Cuts Will Harm Seniors' Access to Physician Care," Press Release, www.ama-assn.org/ama/pub/category/16117.html (accessed April 25, 2007).

9. J. Iglehart, "Linking Compensation to Quality: Medicare Payments to Physicians," *N Engl J Med* 353 (9) (2005): 870–871.

10. Centers for Medicare and Medicaid Services, "Medicare Sustainable Growth Rate," www.cms.hhs.gov/SustainableGRatesConFact/Downloads/sgr2006f.pdf (accessed May 22, 2006).

Additonal Resources

HIPAA—www.cms.hhs.gov/hipaa/hipaa2

ICD-9 and HCPS coding—www.cms.hhs.gov/paymentsystems

Instructions for filing claims—www.cms.hhs.gov/providers/edi/edi5.asp

Medical review—www.cms.hhs.gov/providers/mr

Physician fee schedule—www.cms.hhs.gov/physicians/pfs

Physician Group Practice Project—www.cms.hhs.gov/researchers/demos/PGP.asp

Physicians homepage—www.cms.hhs.gov/physicians

Provider update—www.cms.hhs.gov/providerupdate

Chapter 4

Getting Paid, Part I

Introduction to Coding and the Global Surgery Package

Rebecca Dawson, CPC

Providers use codes to report health services to insurers. The insurers, in turn, use codes to process and pay claims. One analogy is to imagine telling a story using these codes, which are comprised of numbers and/or alpha characters, instead of words. The provider uses codes to write the story about the services provided and the reason for the services. Then, the insurer reads the story and makes payment determinations based on that information.

There is one code set in use by all providers and payers, as mandated by the Health Insurance Portability and Accountability Act (HIPAA). The code set consists of several components, one to report diseases and injuries, others to report services provided. This chapter discusses the code sets applicable to physician services.

Code sets directly applicable to physician services are the International Classification of Diseases, 9th revision, Clinical Modification (ICD-9-CM, or simply ICD-9) Volumes I and II; and the Healthcare Common Procedure Coding System (HCPCS) I and II. HCPCS I is Current Procedural Terminology, or CPT.®* HCPCS II is the Healthcare Common Procedure Coding System, Level II.

Tools for all code sets utilized by providers, whether software or books, should be updated annually as the codes and associated guidelines are revised on an annual basis. It is best not to be "penny wise and pound foolish." Physicians are responsible for using the latest version of codes for

---

* CPT © 2007 American Medical Association. All rights reserved.

billing and reimbursement. Use of correct, current codes can directly affect the practice's bottom line.

ICD-9-CM   ICD-9 codes are used to report illness and injury. Guidelines for the use of these codes are written by the Centers for Medicare and Medicaid Services (CMS) and the National Center for Health Statistics (NCHS). These guidelines are also agreed upon by the American Hospital Association and American Health Information Management Association. Revisions to this coding system are posted on the NCHS Website annually, and are effective October 1 unless otherwise noted by the NCHS.

Volumes I and II of ICD-9 are used by physicians to report their services. Volume I is simply a tabular listing of codes, while Volume II is an alphabetical index. The codes in ICD-9 may be up to five digits long, some of them being alphanumeric.

To assign an ICD-9 code, one first looks for the condition in the alphabetical index. If the condition is not known, the signs or symptoms may be used. Any reference found in the index should be confirmed in the tabular section, where further instructions may be found and completion of coding may be determined. For example, chart documentation shows that the patient has gangrenous cellulitis. To start the process, the coder would look under "cellulitis" in the index. Under "cellulitis," we find "gangrenous, 785.4." Note: The coder with less clear documentation or less experience coding ICD-9 may want to follow instructions in the ICD-9 to "*see also* Abscess," or "*see also* gangrene." It is never a bad idea to check for more information in other areas.

Continuing the example, because we have identified code 785.4, it should be referenced in the tabular section. In the tabular section, we are given definitions, exclusions, and further instructions. At this point, we may also determine whether we have coded to the highest level of specificity—a step that is crucial in ICD-9 coding.

There are many coding conventions associated with ICD-9, including rules for neoplasms and external causes, and for use of the "not elsewhere classified" (NEC) and "not otherwise specified" (NOS) codes. Details can be found in the front of any ICD-9 book or on the NCHS Website. It is important to note that some of the rules differ between physician and facility coding. For example, a physician may never code a condition as "rule out" or "probable" as though it were a definitive diagnosis, while it may be appropriate for a facility to do so. In the physician's case, signs or symptoms would be coded. It is wise to become familiar with the rules of ICD-9 before coding and to use them consistently. Download the ICD-9 rules from the Internet by going to www.cdc.gov and searching for "ICD-9" or by visiting: www.cdc.gov/nchs/data/icd9/icdguide.pdf.

Current Procedural Terminology

Current Procedural Terminology (CPT) codes are used to report medical services and procedures performed by physicians and other qualified providers. The American Medical Association (AMA) publishes CPT codes each fall. Codes generally become effective on the first day of the following year. This system was originally developed by the AMA to make it possible for various health care professionals to communicate in a common language to describe all procedures performed by physicians. A CPT panel consisting of 17 members is responsible for maintaining, revising, and updating the almost 8,000 codes. The AMA nominates 11 members, the Health Care Professionals Advisory Committee nominates 2 members, and the Blue Cross and Blue Shield Association, Health Insurance Association of America, American Hospital Association, and CMS nominate one member each. The panel updates the codes annually, which are then used to update the resource-based relative value scale (RBRVS). The RBRVS assigns a specific value to each CPT code.

There are six sections in the CPT book, along with appendices and an index. The sections are: Evaluation and Management, Anesthesia, Surgery, Radiology, Pathology, and Medicine. Physicians may use any code that accurately describes the service provided; they are not limited to their respective specialty. Physicians may use certain modifiers to alter the meaning of the codes (see Figure 4.1). Unlisted codes are available for instances where an appropriate code, whether modified or not, does not exist.

In using the CPT index, the coder looks for the anatomy or the procedure, rather than the condition of the patient. When utilizing the index, codes should always be confirmed in the referenced section of the book. Each section and subsection of the book will have additional directions that should be read and followed. Coding symbols must be checked before finally assigning the code.

For example, insertion of a central venous device would require checking the index for "insertion," under which we find "venous access device." We further see "central...36560–36566." It should be evident that the code needs to be checked, as there are several. In looking at code 36560, we can identify options not provided in the index. When turning back to the subheading for this portion of the CPT, we can find a list of instructions. Instructions for the pertinent sections and subsections should be read before assigning a code. In this example, we determine that the device has been tunneled on an elderly patient, so we select code 36558. We did not

Figure 4.1   Questions and Answers About CPT Modifiers

What Is a CPT Modifier? Modifiers indicate that a service was altered in some way from the stated CPT descriptor without changing the definition. The AMA CPT modifiers are two-digit numeric codes listed after a procedure code and separated from the CPT code by a hyphen (e.g., 92506-22).

When Should I Use a Modifier? Use a modifier when you need to communicate to the payer that something is atypical about that particular claim.

Can Modifiers Be Used when Billing Medicare as well as Private Health Plans? Medicare carriers and intermediaries vary on the use and acceptance of modifiers. Some Medicare carriers will accept all modifiers listed in the CPT and HCPCS books. (The CPT system does not include all the codes needed to report medical services and supplies, so HCPCS was developed as a second level of codes.) Other carriers may accept only select modifier codes. The same is true for private health plans, so it is important that you check with individual payers regarding their requirements.

Where Can I Find a List of CPT Modifiers? The AMA CPT and HCPCS books, designed for the professional coder, are available through the AMA Press (call 800.621.8335). The *Coders' Desk Reference*, designed for the lay person, is available through Ingenix Companies (call 888.445.8745 or 800.765.6713).

Commonly used modifiers applicable to CPT 2006 codes include:

- -21 Prolonged Evaluation and Management Service. The use of this modifier is indicated when the service provided is prolonged or unusually greater than required for the highest level of evaluation and management (E&M) coding.

- -24 Unrelated Evaluation and Management Service by the Same Physician During a Post-Operative Period. Services submitted with the -24 modifier must be sufficiently documented to establish that the visit was unrelated to the surgery.

- -55 Post-operative Management Only

- -56 Pre-operative Management Only

- -79 Unrelated Procedure or Service by the Same Physician During the Post-Operative Period. The use of CPT modifier -79 is used for unrelated procedures by the same physician during the post-operative period. Unrelated procedures are usually reported using a different ICD-9 diagnosis code.

CPT Modifiers Approved for Hospital Outpatient Use. A few of the most common modifiers approved for hospital outpatient use are:

27 Multiple Outpatient Hospital E/M Encounters on the Same Date

50 Bilateral Procedure

52 Reduced Service

79 Unrelated Procedure or Service by the Same Physician During the Post-Operative Period

91 Repeat Clinical Laboratory Diagnostic Test

---

use fluoroscopic guidance (75998) or ultrasonic guidance (76937) as mentioned in the guidelines, so we would not use those codes for this case.

Evaluation and Management Codes

E&M codes describe visits by physicians and certain other non-physician practitioners. This section of the CPT book has many rules, but CMS has separate documentation guidelines on which it has collaborated with the AMA. One set of guidelines is referenced as 1995, the other as 1997, for the years when the rules were published. Either set is legal, but physicians must not mix these codes; that is, they must use one or the other.

E&M services are divided into categories and some have subcategories. An example of an E&M service category is "Office or Other Outpatient Services." The connected subcategories are "New Patient" and "Established Patient." An example of a rule linked to this category is: a new patient is one who has not received any face-to-face professional services from the physician or another physician of the same specialty in his/her group practice within the past three years. This rule is shared by CPT and CMS.

Service levels must be assigned within each category and/or subcategory and may be selected based on traditional SOAP (subjective, objective, assessment, plan) information, or time. In any case, each visit must have a chief complaint to document the reason for the visit.

There are specific requirements for selecting the code based on time. To code based on time, counseling and coordination of care must have been over 50 percent of the service provided. Counseling and coordination of care must be done face-to-face in the outpatient setting, but may include unit or floor time devoted to that patient in the inpatient setting. Only the physician's time counts, in any location—that of residents or ancillary staff does not go toward billing.

Counseling includes discussion with the patient of test results, impressions, recommendations of additional studies, prognosis, risks and benefits of management options, instructions, importance of compliance, and so forth. Unit or floor time (inpatient only) may include time spent reviewing the patient's chart, reviewing test results, and communicating with other professionals.

Times associated with E&M codes are approximate. You will find that emergency room visits do not have associated times due to the nature of this type of visit. Some codes are solely based on time, such as critical care services and hospital discharge day management. When documenting time-based services, it must be clear that the majority of the time was spent counseling.

Example: An established patient comes in to discuss results of tests. The physician spends 40 minutes with the patient, all of which was spent counseling. Documentation might look like this: "I spent 40 minutes with Mrs. Smith today, going over the results of her MRI and CT scans, my impressions, and treatment options that include surgery, watchful waiting, and medication. At this point, she has decided to take the watchful-waiting option and will return to my clinic in 6 months for follow-up."

When coding by SOAP elements, it becomes a little more complicated. First, SOAP translates into history ("S"), exam ("O") and medical decisionmaking ("AP"). These three key components are described in more detail in the following sections.

The History Component

The history component has three elements: history of present illness, review of systems, and past/family/social history (PFSH). Within the history of present illness, there are eight other elements: location, duration, severity, modifying factors, timing, context, quality, and associated signs/symptoms. The review of systems consists of the questions asked patients regarding their condition or pertinent other conditions they may have or have had. This review may be inventoried on a form completed by the patient. PFSH should be self-explanatory. It consists of personal history of surgery or hospitalizations, medicines taken, history of illnesses experienced by living or deceased family members, and work and social habits. This is not a complete list, but provides a general idea. These three elements together determine the history level (see Table 4.1).

The Exam Component

The exam component is a little simpler than the history component, if using the 1995 guidelines (Tables 4.2 and 4.3). The number of body areas and/or organ systems examined, and the extent of the exam determine the exam level. While somewhat vague, the 1995 guidelines are often seen as more practical than the 1997 guidelines. The 1997 exam guidelines are based on a bullet-point system where credit is given for each bullet-point performed, depending on areas designated specifically for each exam. While some parts of the exam performed may not be given credit by the guidelines, required elements may not be medically necessary; this makes it difficult to assign appropriate credit. However, examinations documented by these guidelines may be easier to quantify in the event of an audit.

The 1997 exam guidelines consist of one general multisystem examination and 10 specialty examinations: cardiovascular; eye; ear, nose and throat; respiratory; genitourinary; skin; musculoskeletal; neurological; psychiatric; hematologic and lymphatic; and immunologic. There are too many to list; find the complete guidelines by searching the CMS Website at www.cms.hhs.gov for the exact phrase "Documentation Guidelines for E&M Services" (use quotation marks to narrow your search).

Table 4.1 E&M Exams: The History Component

Chief Complaint		
History of Present Illness: 8 Elements	**Review of Systems: 10 or More Systems**	**Past, Family, Social History**
Location	Constitutional	**Past:**
Quality	Eyes	■ Surgical history
Severity	Ears, nose, mouth, throat	■ Hospitalizations
Duration	Cardiovascular	■ Medications
Timing	Respiratory	**Family:**
Context	Gastrointestinal	■ Illnesses of family members
Modifying factors	Genitourinary	**Social:**
Associated signs and symptoms	Integumentary	■ Tobacco use
	Musculoskeletal	■ Smoking
	Neurological	■ Alcohol use
	Hematologic and lymphatic	■ Illicit drug use
	Allergic and immunologic	■ Work
	Psychiatric	■ Education
	Endocrine	■ Travel

Source: Rebecca Dawson. Adapted from Centers for Medicare and Medicaid Services, "Evaluation and Management Services Guide," www.cms.hhs.gov/MLNProducts/downloads/eval_mgmt_serv_guide.pdf (accessed April 23, 2007).

The Medical Decisionmaking Component

Medical decisionmaking is another component with three elements—risk, data, and management options. Risk is defined by a table from which one simply selects the highest level that is pertinent. Briefly, data elements are made up of tests and their results, discussion with others, and old records. The tables shown in the section "Using the 1995 Guidelines" show these data elements. Points are given for each data element described. Some elements are assigned one point, others two. Points may be given only once in any given area. For example, ordering an X-ray is worth one point. If two X-rays are ordered, it is still worth only one point. Finally, management options are defined by whether:

■ The problem is new to the physician, and whether additional workup is being planned;

■ Known problems are improving or worsening; or

■ The problem is self-limited or minor, and the number of problems.

Table 4.2   E&M Exams: The 1995 Examination Components

Organ Systems		Body Areas
Constitutional	Genitourinary	Head, face
Eyes	Musculoskeletal	Neck
Ears, nose, mouth, throat	Skin	Chest, breast, axillae
Cardiovascular	Neurological	Abdomen
Respiratory	Psychiatric	Genitalia, groin, buttocks
Gastrointestinal	Hematologic, lymphatic, immune	Back, spine
		Each extremity

Source: Rebecca Dawson. Adapted from Centers for Medicare and Medicaid Services, "Evaluation and Management Services Guide," www.cms.hhs.gov/MLNProducts/downloads/eval_mgmt_serv_guide.pdf (accessed April 23, 2007).

Table 4.3   The 1995 Exam Levels

Exam Level	Required Elements
Problem focused	Limited exam of the affected body area or organ system
Expanded problem focused	Limited exam of the affected body area or organ system, plus other symptomatic or related organ systems (up to seven systems)
Detailed	Extended exam of the affected body area or organ system, plus other symptomatic or related organ systems (up to seven systems)
Comprehensive	Complete exam of a single organ system or general multisystem exam (eight or more organ systems)

Source: Rebecca Dawson. Adapted from Centers for Medicare and Medicaid Services, "Evaluation and Management Services Guide," www.cms.hhs.gov/MLNProducts/downloads/eval_mgmt_serv_guide.pdf (accessed April 23, 2007).

Table 4.4   Data Options: E&M Options Using the 1995 Guidelines

Data	Points
Review or order of clinical lab tests	1
Review or order of radiology tests	1
Review or order of medical tests (e.g., EKG)	1
Discuss test results with performing physician	1
Decision to get old records or history from someone other than the patient	1
Review and summarize old records or get history from someone other than the patient or discuss the case with another health care provider	2
Personal visualization of image, specimen, or tracing itself, not just reading the report	2

Source: Rebecca Dawson. Adapted from Centers for Medicare and Medicaid Services, "Evaluation and Management Services Guide," www.cms.hhs.gov/MLNProducts/downloads/eval_mgmt_serv_guide.pdf (accessed April 23, 2007).

Table 4.5   E&M Options Using the 1995 Guidelines

Problems to Examining Physician	Number of Problems	Points
Self-limited or minor	Maximum allowed = 2	1
Established, stable, or improving	No maximum	1
Established, worsening, or not responding	No maximum	2
New, no additional workup planned	Maximum allowed = 1	3
New, additional workup planned	Maximum = 1	4

Source: Rebecca Dawson. Adapted from Centers for Medicare and Medicaid Services, "Evaluation and Management Services Guide," www.cms.hhs.gov/MLNProducts/downloads/eval_mgmt_serv_guide.pdf (accessed April 23, 2007).

Two of these three elements must be at the same level, or exceeded, to select the level of medical decisionmaking.

Find the official table of risk for the 1995 guidelines by searching the CMS Website at www.cms.hhs.gov using the exact phrase "Documentation Guidelines for E&M Services" (use quotation marks to narrow your search). Select the downloadable guidelines for 1995.

Using the 1995 Guidelines

To understand how the 1995 guidelines work, refer to Table 4.4 and Table 4.5 to see how they are used in the following example.

"Mrs. Jones came to me for care of a possible hernia. She has had pain in the right inguinal area for the past 6 months. Highest level of pain has been a 5, on a scale of 1 to 10. At first, she tried a heating pad, but it did not help. She then saw her family doctor who suggested she see a surgeon."

Chief complaint:	Possible hernia
Location:	RT inguinal region
Duration:	6 months
Severity:	5 out of 10
Modifying factor:	Heating pad

"Mrs. Jones has not had any constipation or diarrhea, no weight loss; is diabetic, diet controlled."

Review of systems:	GI, constitutional, endocrine

"Mrs. Jones has no past history of surgery, does not smoke."

Past and Social History

History of present illness level:	Extended, due to 4 elements
Review of systems level:	Extended, due to 3 elements
PFSH level:	Pertinent, due to 2 elements, new patient
Overall history level:	Detailed

History Levels

The following chart shows the various E&M elements recorded in the examination of Mrs. Jones:

HPI	Brief (1–3)	Brief (1–3)	Extended (4+)	Extended (4+)
ROS	None	Problem pertinent (1)	Extended (2–9)	Complete (10+)
PFSH	None	None	Pertinent (1)	Complete (2 or 3)
Level	Problem focused	Expanded problem focused	Detailed	Comprehensive

"Mrs. Jones is a 50-year-old white female who appears to be of stated age, in no acute distress. Her abdomen is not tender, not distended, no hepatosplenomegaly, no scars, positive bowel sounds, no guarding. She has an inguinal hernia on the right. No hernia is found on the left."

Exam:	Abdomen, extended, plus constitutional
Exam level:	Detailed

"My recommendation is surgical repair by laparoscopic method. We discussed the risks and benefits of surgery and the alternatives, and she agrees to have the surgery scheduled."

Data:	Straightforward, as there is none
Management:	Moderate, as it is a new problem and no additional workup is planned
Risk:	Moderate, due to elective major surgery
Decisionmaking:	Moderate

Medical Decision-making Levels

As this example shows, taking a detailed history and conducting a detailed exam, plus a moderate level of medical decisionmaking for this new patient, can be described as a "detailed new patient visit." Find the

Management options	Minimal (1)	Limited (2)	Multiple (3)	Extensive (4)
Risk	Minimal	Low	Moderate	High
Data	Minimal (1)	Limited (2)	Moderate (3)	Extensive (4)
Level	Straightforward	Low	Moderate	High

complete guidelines by searching the CMS Website at www.cms.hhs.gov for the exact phrase "Documentation Guidelines for E&M Services" (use quotation marks to narrow your search).

Modifiers

Find modifiers and their descriptions in the appendices of the CPT book. Use them to change the story told by the physician and give more information to the payer. Some modifiers apply only to E&M codes, while others pertain only to procedures or tests. An example of an E&M-only modifier is modifier -24, which indicates unrelated E&M service during the post-op period. It is used when the patient is seen during the regular post-op period for a condition unrelated to the surgery, or for treatment of the underlying condition, or counseling regarding an additional course of treatment. A surgery-only modifier is modified -52, which indicates reduced services. It is used when only a portion of a service described by a specific CPT code is performed.

The Healthcare Common Procedural Coding System

The HCPCS was established in 1978 with the intent to standardize a coding system that describes various items and services provided in the process of delivering health care. The goal was to have uniform, orderly, and consistent methodology in processing Medicare, Medicaid, and other insurance claims. The HCPCS became mandatory with the passage of HIPAA. The HCPCS has two major classifications: Level I, which is made up of the CPT-4 numeric AMA coding system familiar to physicians; and Level II, which has identifiers for various products, supplies, and services. CMS has a new council on technology and innovation, which was established as part of the Medicare Prescription Drug, Improvement and Modernization Act (MMA), that oversees all activities related to coverage, coding, and payment processes affecting new technology and procedures.

HCPCS II

HCPCS II is a component of the Healthcare Common Procedural Coding System dedicated to products, supplies, and services not in the CPT book. The codes are alphanumeric and are maintained by CMS. Like HCPCS I, it is revised annually in the fall with changes becoming effective the first of the following year. HCPCS II codes are classified by product or service similarity. Some examples of HCPCS II services are casting materials, dental services, some temporary codes, and so forth. Find more information on HCPCS II codes by searching the CMS Website at www.cms.hhs.gov for the exact phrase "HCPCS—General Information" (use quotation marks to narrow your search).

Figure 4.2   Questions and Answers About Global Surgery Billing

What Is a Global Surgery Fee? A global surgery fee includes all necessary services performed by the physician before, during, and after a surgical procedure. Medicare payment for a given surgical procedure includes applicable pre-operative and intra-operative services, complications, and post-operative care.

How Long Is the Global Period? Major surgery has a 90-day follow-up period. Minor procedures have a 0- or 10-day follow-up period. Some procedures (most radiology interventional procedures) have no global period, which means that any office visits following the procedure can be billed.

What Are the Components of a Global Period? The components included in the global surgical fee are:

1. *Pre-operative visits.* These visits are defined as the visits one (1) day before or the same day as a surgical procedure. Preoperative visits are not paid separately unless the physician indicates that the service was a significant, separately identifiable service (modifier 25) or the service was a decision for major surgery (modifier 57).

2. *Intra-operative services.* These services are those that are normally a usual and necessary part of a surgical procedure. This is the fee for the surgical service itself.

3. *Complications following surgery.* Under Medicare rules, this is all additional medical or surgical services required of the surgeon within 10 (minor surgery) or 90 days (major surgery) of the surgery because of complications that do not require additional trips to the operative room. Services are allowed if the provider indicates that the procedure was staged (modifier 58), or a return trip to the operating room (modifier 78). If the E/M service is unrelated to the surgery, e.g., treatment of the underlying condition or additional treatment planning, modifier 24 is allowed. Surgery with 000 global days that are billed with one of the above modifiers may not be appropriate.

4. *Post-operative visits.* These services are defined as follow-up visits during the post-operative period of surgery that is related to recovery from surgery. These services can be allowed if the provider indicates that the visit was an unrelated service during the post-operative period (modifier 24).

The Global Surgery Package

The global surgery package, which states what is and is not included in the cost of a surgery, is defined somewhat differently by the AMA in its CPT book than it is by the CMS guidelines. It addresses issues such as complications, dressing changes, post-operative visits, and so forth. For the purposes of this chapter, we will focus on the CMS guidelines. (See Figure 4.2 for more information).

Surgical procedures may have a 0-, 10- or 90-day global period assigned to them. An example of a 0-day procedure might be insertion of a non-tunneled central line. A 10-day global service might be removal of a benign lesion. The actual period is 11 days, including the day of the procedure, and 10 days after. Major surgeries have 90-day global periods, which are actually 92 days—the day before, the day of the procedure, and 90 days after. Any E&M services provided on the day of or day before a procedure are generally not payable. During the global period, global package guidelines apply.

An example of services included in the global surgery package, as defined by CMS, include post-op wound checks; dressing changes; removal of sutures, tubes, or drains; non-operative treatment of complications; and pain management. Generally any E&M service related to the procedure done on the same day of surgery, or after the decision to perform surgery, is included. Services excluded from the global surgery package include:

- E&M visits that result in the decision to perform surgery;

- Visits unrelated to the diagnosis for which the procedure is to be performed; and

- Visits for treatment of an underlying condition or for an added course of treatment and treatment of complications that require a return trip to the operating room.

Find complete global surgery package guidelines on the CMS Website at www.cms.hhs.gov by searching for the exact phrase "Medicare Claims Processing Manual" (use quotation marks to narrow your search). Look for Section 40 of the manual.

National Correct Coding Initiative

The National Correct Coding Initiative, NCCI, or simply CCI, is a set of edits used by insurers to prevent payment of services that should be components of other services provided during the same patient encounter. Billing for component parts of a service, rather than billing the comprehensive service, is called *unbundling*. Unbundling of services could result in overpayment of claims based on payment guidelines, which may, in turn, result in accusations of false claims. These edits were developed by CMS and can be found on the CMS Website at www.cms.hhs.gov by searching for the exact phrase "National Correct Coding Initiative Edits" (use quotation marks to narrow your search).

An example of a bundled service is an exploratory laparotomy done during the same operative session as an open colectomy. This is because the laparotomy is considered a component procedure of the colectomy. Another example of bundled services is a cholecystectomy and cholecystoenterostomy because one is mutually exclusive to the other. It is possible to appropriately unbundle some of these services, where allowed by CCI and the circumstances. This is done by using a CPT modifier to indicate a distinct procedure service. To qualify as a distinct service, services must be provided at separate sessions or encounters; must be different procedures or surgeries; must be on different sites or organ systems; or be separate incisions, lesions, or injuries that would not ordinarily be encountered or performed on the same day. Use caution when unbundling services as this is often done inappropriately and, therefore, watched by CMS and other payers.

Conclusion   Several coding books and guidelines are necessary to assign the correct codes and bill a claim appropriately. Physicians should educate themselves and become familiar with these matters or hire certified coders to read their documentation and assign codes for them. Even if physicians choose to assign codes, it is helpful to have qualified staff on the billing team to review coding before it is billed, or at least to handle denials on the back end and audits when they arise. In any case, it is ultimately the physician's responsibility, as it is he/she who signs the CMS-1500 billing form and attests that all services billed were provided and medically necessary. It is the physician who stands to lose from an incorrect or non-compliant claim. Staying in compliance is a full-time job and should be a part of daily operations.

Chapter 5

Getting Paid, Part II:

The Resource-Based Relative Value Scale, Medicare Physician Fee Schedule, and Other Payment Mechanisms

Prior to 1992, reimbursement to health care professionals and hospitals was based on "customary, prevailing, and reasonable" charges. As part of the restructuring effort initiated by primary care specialties, Congress passed legislation as part of the Omnibus Budget Reconciliation Act of 1989. The Department of Health and Human Services (HHS) was instructed to reward "cognitive" physicians by redistributing Medicare payments away from procedural-oriented specialties to these caregivers under a revenue-neutral method. The Health Care Financing Administration (HCFA), which is now the Centers for Medicare and Medicaid Services (CMS), revised reimbursement for physician services by implementing the resource-based relative value scale (RBRVS). The actual work scale was developed by Hsiao and his colleagues at Harvard University starting in 1985 by expressing almost 7,000 services in the Current Procedural Terminology (CPT®)[*] system as a work value, and assigning them a relative value unit or RVU.[1] These work units were to be reviewed every 5 years to address under- or over-evaluation.

Calculating RVUs

Each RVU has three components:

1. Physician work (WRVU): time, intensity of service, and technical skill required to provide the service. The WRVU represents approximately 52 percent of the total RVU;

---

[*]CPT © 2007 American Medical Association. All rights reserved.

2. Practice expenses (PE-RVU): rent, staff salaries, and supplies. The PE-RVU represents approximately about 44 percent of the total RVU; and

3. Malpractice premiums (M-RVU). The M-RVU represents approximately 4 percent of the total RVU.

The RVUs of each component are then modified by a geographic practice cost index (GPCI). The adjusted RVUs are then multiplied by a national conversion factor (CF), $37.89 in 2007, to come up with actual reimbursement. Whereas practice expenses and malpractice overhead were calculated initially based on historic numbers, physician work was assumed to be the product of time needed to perform a CPT service multiplied by the intensity of that service.

A WRVU is the largest component of the RVU. It is a unit of measure used to indicate the amount of effort (time, intensity of effort, and technical skills) required in performing a particular service relative to other services. The WRVU is not necessarily doubled or tripled simply because double or triple the amount of time was spent on a patient compared to another patient. As an example, an office visit lasting 20 minutes may be counted as one WRVU, whereas a 35-minute physical examination of a complicated cardiac patient may be counted as 3 or 4 WRVUs.

Example:

Components: Work (WRVU):	Time, skill, stress
Practice expense (PE-RVU):	Practice costs excluding malpractice insurance and physician compensation
Malpractice (M-RVU):	Cost of malpractice insurance

Example:

CPT-99243 (level 3 office or outpatient consult, non-facility setting)

	RVU	GPCI	Product
WRVU	1.88	1.0	1.88
PE-RVU	1.41	0.934	1.32
M-RVU	0.13	0.96	0.12
Total	3.42	2.894	3.32

If the CF is $37.8975, then CPT-99243 will be reimbursed at 3.32 times 37.8975 resulting in $125.82.

RVUs are used as the basis for reimbursement of physician services by Medicare and by many third-party payers. The physician fee schedule conversion factor is updated each year by the percentage change in the Medicare Economic Index, which measures the weighted average price change for various inputs involved with producing physician services. The fee schedule update is adjusted by a performance adjustment factor that compares actual and target expenditures. CMS has estimated that, pending action by Congress, the physician fee schedule conversion factor in 2007 would be $36.1542, a 4.6 percent reduction from 2006. (Note: In late 2006, the 109th Congress took action to prevent the scheduled reduction.)

Who Reviews and Updates RVUs?

The Physician Payment Review Commission was identified by Congress as the primary advisory committee to review all matters related to RBRVS and any adjustments necessary. Congress then approves the conversion factor each year based on the projected inflation rate, Medicare enrollment changes, projected vs. actual claim volumes, and other pertinent events that influence the Medicare Part B budget.

Also charged to review RVUs is the Medicare Payment Advisory Commission (MedPAC), an independent federal body that Congress established in 1997 to analyze access, quality of care, and other issues affecting Medicare. The process involves a review and feedback from the American Medical Association RVU Committee as well as other stakeholders; publishing a proposed rule asking for public comment; followed by a final rule and implementation, which takes 12 months to 18 months. The WRVU data is submitted to the University Health System Consortium and the Association of American Medical Colleges by the consortium members. A statistical analysis determines values such as mean, median, and percentiles.

Congress also requests MedPAC's input on a variety of issues, appearance before hearings, participation in briefings for Congressional committees and staff, and solicits comments on important issues related to Medicare beneficiaries. Recent reports have dealt with payment for long-term care hospitals, inpatient rehabilitation, hospital and physician reimbursement, inpatient and outpatient prospective payment systems, specialty hospitals, pay-for-performance programs, reviewing existing WRVUs and home health services. MedPAC also advises Congress on payments to health plans participating in the Medicare Advantage program, as well as in Medicare's traditional fee-for-service programs. MedPAC consists of 17 members appointed by the Comptroller General, representing diverse sectors of health care, and supported by analysts with backgrounds in economics, health policy, or medicine. The Comptroller General, who heads the U.S. Government Accountability Office, has the authority to name new commission members to represent all sectors of the health care environment as well as consumers.

Non-RVU Activities

Many of the activities provided by faculty in medical schools and universities do not generate RVUs. These include research, teaching, and publishing. In this situation, if pay is based on activities other than RVUs, production reports may display the work in RVU equivalents to include any dollars brought in by research grants. Providing direct or indirect reward mechanisms for the non-clinical activities of physicians is less commonly seen at private medical practices. However, a number of hospital-affiliated medical practices do attempt to encourage and reward physicians for taking on additional roles in administration, committee work, teambuilding, satellite offices, and other outreach activities. For example, if a physician must travel an hour each day to work at an outreach location, the practice might establish a WRVU credit for that travel time. The credit could be based on the WRVUs of services the physician might have typically performed in the same amount of time if stationed at the practice's main office.[2]

Sustainable Growth Rate Formula

The use of sustainable growth rate (SGR) targets is intended to control the growth in aggregate Medicare expenditures for physicians' services.[3] The targets are not said to be direct limits on expenditures, meaning that payments for services are not withheld if the SGR target is exceeded by actual expenditures. However, in practical terms, if target expenditures on physician spending in one year are exceeded, the SGR formula takes this into account for the next year's update. The Social Security Act requires the secretary of HHS to make available to MedPAC and the public by March 1 every year, an estimate of the SGR and CF applicable to Medicare payments for physicians' services for the following year, and the data underlying these estimates. As indicated in chapter 3 on Medicare, the SGR has so far been linked to the national economy.

The following factors are used in the calculation of the SGR:

- Estimated percent change in fees for physician services;

- Estimated change in the average number of Medicare fee-for-service beneficiaries; and

- Estimated 10-year average annual growth in real gross domestic product (GDP) per capita.

Prior to the Medicare Prescription Drug, Improvement and Modernization Act (MMA), the SGR was calculated using estimated projected growth in real GDP per capita. However, the MMA amended the statute to require the secretary to calculate the SGR using the 10-year annual average growth in real GDP per capita. GDP numbers are based on estimates by the Bureau of Economic Analysis of the Department of Commerce,[4] and population numbers are taken from the home page for the Census Bureau.[5] Both these numbers are then used for calculation of real GDP estimates. MedPAC has expressed its opinion (and concurs with physicians) that the SGR formula is flawed and has plans to address the inequality in the formula.

Diagnosis-Related Groups

Reimbursement to hospitals for in-patients by Medicare and Medicaid is based on the RBRVS in the form of diagnosis-related groups (DRGs). DRGs are groupings of conditions affecting about 25 organ systems further broken down into 538 medical groupings, which Medicare assumes are similar in the resources consumed for treatment purposes. Since 1986, hospitals have been reimbursed under a prospective payment system (PPS) that pays hospitals a fixed rate. It creates an incentive to keep the hospital fixed cost below the reimbursement rate. Medicare utilizes "charges" on hospital claims to set payment weights. An abdominal aortic aneurysm repair may have a "weight" three or four times that of pneumonia, indicating the amount of resources consumed in the care of the aneurysm patient. However, the charges do not accurately reflect true cost of the care rendered.

Recent Changes to Move to Cost-Based DRGs

There is a move by CMS to pay hospital-based services on approximate cost rather than charges. Sloane has summarized some of the proposed changes as follows:[6]

- Provide a full market update for hospitals worth about $3.3 billion;

- Improve recognition of severity of illness as part of DRG reform;

- Shift payments (approximately $1.6 billion a year) from very profitable illnesses such as coronary artery intervention to under-compensated illnesses such as pneumonia; and

- Implement a new diagnosis coding system (ICD-10-CM) that would lead to more accuracy in reimbursement policies.

The American Hospital Association, as Sloan points out, has in principle expressed support for reforms, but it opposes changes that may hurt hospital profitability.[7] CMS has also proposed a new inpatient prospective payment system for 2007 as an update on the 2003 MMA. In the MMA, hospitals were required to report on 10 clinical quality measures to qualify for full payment of updates for inflation. For 2007, CMS is proposing asking hospitals to pledge to report on 11 (for a total of 21) quality indicators retroactive to January 2006. These new indicators would include measures related to heart attacks, heart failure, pneumonia, and surgical infection prevention. Although reporting is still voluntary, inpatient acute care hospitals that do not report will receive a 2 percent reduction in their annual Medicare fee schedule update.

Outpatient Prospective System for Hospitals

The Balanced Budget Act of 1997 (section 4523), and the follow-up 1999 Balanced Budget Refinement Act give CMS authority to implement a PPS under Medicare. Payment to hospitals for outpatients is based on ambulatory payment classifications (APCs).[7] Most outpatient procedures have a pre-assigned APC code that groups together services which are similar with respect to resource utilization and require a fixed payment rate. To be profitable, health care systems utilize different strategies to deal with inpatient (DRG-based) reimbursement vs. outpatients. Within some constraints and, in general (excluding outliers), because payments are fixed for in-patients, the goal is to reduce costs by reducing the amount of resources used by the patient. For outpatients, in general, provided the cost of providing services does not exceed reimbursement, any additional volume is bound to be profitable.

Outpatient Tests

Outpatient tests are reimbursed for the technical or professional components separately or together as a global payment. Inpatient studies, such as ultrasound tests, are reimbursed for the professional component only, as the technical part is included in the DRG payment to the hospital.

References

1. W.C. Hsaio, and others, "The Resource-Based Relative Value Scale: Toward the Development of an Alternative Physician Payment System," *JAMA* 258 (1987): 799–802.

2. B. Johnson and D. Walker Keegan, *Physician Compensation Plans.* Englewood, CO: Medical Group Management Association (2006).

3. Centers for Medicare and Medicaid Services, "Estimated Sustainable Growth Rate and Conversion Factor, for Medicare Payments to Physicians in 2006," Dec. 21, 2005, www.cms.hhs.gov/ SustainableGRatesConFact/Downloads/sgr2006f.pdf (accessed May 22, 2006).

4. Bureau of Economic Analysis, "Gross Domestic Product," www.bea.gov/bea/dn/home/gdp.htm (accessed May 22, 2006).

5. U.S. Census Bureau, www.census.gov (accessed May 22, 2006).

6. T. Sloane "The Devil's in the Dollars," *Modern Healthcare* 36 (25) (2006): 33

7. *Federal Register*, April 7, 2000, 65 FR 18434, implemented Aug. 1, 2000.

Part 2

A Guide to Accounting and Finance

Chapter 6

Financial Statements: What They Are and What They Tell Us

E. Ann Gabriel, PhD, CPA

Financial accounting identifies, measures, and communicates financial information to investors, creditors, suppliers, and other parties who do business with an economic entity. We say *economic entity* because financial reporting is essentially the same whether the entity is a corporation of any form, a partnership of any form, or a sole practitioner. The information provided to these interested parties must be useful for investment and/or credit decisions. To serve this purpose, financial accounting must provide information that is both relevant to the decision to be made, and of sufficient accuracy to be reliable for decisionmaking purposes. In addition, because investors or creditors may have to make decisions between two entities, accounting information must also be comparable and consistent across all entities.

To ensure that financial accounting reports can provide information to investors and creditors useful for decisionmaking (that is, relevant, reliable, comparable, and consistent), the accounting profession has developed a set of principles, standards, and procedures called *generally accepted accounting principles* or GAAP. These rules are established by boards of knowledgeable practitioners. The key boards are:

The Securities and Exchange Commission (SEC). A federal agency with oversight powers. All publicly traded companies must follows rules established by the SEC. At the present time, the SEC has deferred to the Financial Accounting Standards Board to set accounting rules;

The Financial Accounting Standards Board (FASB). A private-sector agency that establishes and improves reporting standards. Public and private companies are subject to rules set by the FASB, if they want to be in compliance with GAAP; and

The International Accounting Standards Board (IASB). An international body set up to achieve consistency in accounting standards. While companies in the United States follow the U.S. GAAP, the FASB and IASB are working to bring consistency and comparability to U.S. and international accounting standards.

Following these rules and GAAP, the accountant prepares financial statements to provide information to the users of the financial statements.

The Financial Statements

There are three basic financial statements that must be provided to users of the financial information: the balance sheet, the income statement, and the statement of cash flows. The balance sheet presents a picture of the entity at a specific point in time. It is called a balance sheet because the assets (the resources the entity has to support its operations) must be equal to the liabilities (what it owes its suppliers and creditors) plus owners' equity (what the owners have contributed to the entity and what is available for them).

The income statement and the statement of cash flows cover a period of time and provide the link between balance sheets. The income statements present all the revenue earned during the period and all the expenses incurred to earn those revenues. The *net income* for the period on the income statement is the link between the owners' equity on the period end balance sheet and the one for the previous period.

Notice that nothing was said about cash. This is where the statement of cash flows comes in. The statement of cash flows tells the reader of the financial statements how cash was generated during the period and how it was spent. The net increase (decrease) in cash for the period is the link between the cash on the period-end balance sheet and the one for the previous period. For example, Anderson, Bailey, and Comstock Medical Corporation (ABC Medical Corporation) financed the leasehold improvements for its new office from the local bank. As part of the loan agreement, the bank is to receive ABC Medical Corporation's financial statements at the end of each quarter and at the end of the year. The accompanying financial statements were supplied by ABC Medical Corporation's accountant (see Figures 6.1, 6.2 and 6.3). As its name implies, ABC Medical Corporation is a corporation. The legal structure of a corporation has the advantage of limited liability, but the disadvantage of double taxation of the practice's profit. A detailed discussion of options for the legal structure of a practice is found in chapter 1, "Business Structures in Health Care" in Volume 1 of The Smarter Physician Series (©2007 MGMA).

Figure 6.1   Anderson, Bailey, and Comstock Medical Corporation Balance Sheet—for the Year Ended Dec. 31, 2006

Assets			Liabilities and Owners' Equity		
Current Assets			**Current Liabilities**		
Cash		$188,495	Accounts Payable		$25,311
Accounts Receivable			Salaries Payable		15,504
Patients	$31,638		Accrued Income Taxes		54,340
Insurance Companies	84,740		Notes Payable—Current Portion		90,118
Total	116,378				
Less: Allowance for Doubtful Accounts	(9,310)				
Accounts Receivable, Net		107,068			
Drug and Clinic Supplies		11,813			
Prepaids		10,866			
Total Current Assets		318,242	Total Current Liabilities		185,273
Property and Equipment					
Professional Equipment	83,211		Notes Payable, less Current Portion	$443,806	
Furniture and Fixtures	201,521		Net Long-Term Liabilities		443,806
Autos	147,572				
Leasehold Improvements	552,051				
Computer Equipment	91,704				
Office Equipment	52,144		**Total Liabilities**		629,079
	1,128,203				
Less: Accumulated Depreciation	(546,891)				
Total Property and Equipment		581,312	**Owners' Equity**		
			Common Stock, par value $1	1,000	
			5,000 Shares Authorized		
			1,000 Shares Issued and Outstanding		
Other Assets			Additional Paid-In Capital	93,976	
Deposits and Other Assets	37,997		Retained Earnings	213,496	
Total Other Assets		37,997	**Total Owners' Equity**		308,472
Total Assets		$937,551	**Total Liabilities and Owners' Equity**		$937,551

© 2007 Ann Gabriel

NOTE: This sample balance sheet appears in Appendix E on the CD so that you can use it as a template.

The Balance Sheet

As just mentioned, the balance sheet (Figure 6.1) for ABC Medical Corporation is a picture of the practice at a specific point in time, in this case Dec. 31, 2006. The three major sections of the balance sheet (explored in more depth in the next sections) are:

- *Current assets and liabilities.* These resources are used in the day-to-day operation of the practice;

- *Property and equipment, and other long-term assets.* Property and equipment are those tangible assets used over two or more years that are needed to provide a place to meet patients and the equipment to care for them. Other long-term assets could include general costs of doing business such as deposits required by building leases or health care insurance providers; and

- *Long-term liabilities and owners' equity.* Long-term liabilities are generally financing received from outside sources such as bank loans. Owners' equity is the financing provided by the physician–owners of the practice.

Current Assets

Current assets are resources that will become cash or used to produce cash in the next 12 months. ABC Medical Corporation's balance sheet presents current assets common to most medical practices. As can be seen on ABC Medical Corporation's balance sheet, current assets are listed from the most liquid to the least liquid.

Cash is always the first current asset listed. In some cases, the practice may be accumulating cash for a major purchase. Instead of leaving cash in a non-interest bearing account, a practice may place excess cash in short-term investments to earn interest. In such cases, the caption on the balance sheet may read "Cash and short-term investments."

The next item in the current asset section is accounts receivable. Accounts receivable represents amounts due to the practice for services already provided. In general, amounts due from different types of payers are listed separately. In the case of ABC Medical Corporation, amounts are due from patients and from insurance companies. For a variety of reasons, all of the accounts receivable may not be collected by the practice. For example, an insurance company may deny coverage and the patient may not be able to pay for the care received. To cover such cases, the practice may establish an allowance for doubtful accounts. Accountants will review the accounts receivable to determine how long each has been outstanding and calculate an allowance based on the practice's experience with collecting past due accounts.

Most practices also keep supplies on hand for examination room use and patient treatments. Finally, some expenses may be paid in advance, or prepaids. For example, office leases may be paid a quarter in advance. In a similar manner, insurance premiums may be paid for a year. Many other assets could be categorized as current. The key is that the asset will become cash or be used to produce cash within the next 12 months.

Current Liabilities

Current liabilities are the counterpart of current assets in that they will require the expenditure of cash in the next 12 months. Accounts payable are amounts due to vendors or suppliers; they are generally payable in 30 days or less. Other labels are often given to certain types of accounts payable to be more descriptive. For example, ABC Medical Corporation's balance sheet reports salaries payable, which represents amounts owed to ABC Medical Corporation's employees for work already completed. Many practices will also report accrued expenses. Accrued items are similar to payables in that they will require expenditure of cash within 12 months. However, accrued expenses are not currently due or do not need to be paid within 30 days, as is the case of payables.

ABC Medical Corporation's balance sheet reports accrued income taxes. As ABC Medical Corporation's accountant prepares financial statements each month, he/she records the income taxes that will be due on the income earned in the month, even though income taxes are not due until three months after the practice's year end. The last item reported in current liabilities is notes payable–current portion. Technically, the term *notes payable* is incorrect because notes are usually paid over several years. However, that is the convention used in financial reporting. Notes payable–current portion is exactly what it sounds like. It is the part of the long-term debt that will be paid in the next 12 months.

Looking at ABC Medical Corporation's balance sheet, one can see that ABC Medical Corporation expects to collect $318,242 and expend $159,962 during the next 12 months. Having adequate cash to run the practice for the next 12 months does not appear to be a problem.

Property and Equipment

Property and equipment include the long-term tangible assets used to provide service to patients and operate the practice. Unlike current assets, which are expected to be converted to cash within 12 months, property and equipment are expected to be used to generate professional service revenue for many years. Property and equipment are presented by major category at the original cost of the asset. This provides information to the reader of the financial statements as to how much as been invested to support the ongoing operations of the practice. Each asset category usually has an expected useful life, or an expected length of time that it can be used before it needs to be replaced. The cost of the property and equipment is charged against the income of the practice over its useful life.

On the balance sheet, the cumulative charge over time is reported as accumulated depreciation. It is reported as a negative amount to be subtracted from the total cost of the property and equipment. Accumulated depreciation and the related depreciation expense are discussed in greater detail in chapter 7, "Using Financial Statements to Make Decisions." It is important to note that the actual cost, as well as the accumulated depreciation, is reported on the balance sheet. ABC Medical Corporation has property and equipment with an original cost of $1,128,203, and accumulated depreciation of $546,821. The reader can tell that, on average, about half of the useful life of the assets has passed and that ABC Medical Corporation may need to invest in new assets in the not-too-distant future. This may mean that ABC Medical Corporation may need to borrow money or the physician–owners may have to increase their investment.

Other Long-Term Assets

Other long-term assets is a catch-all category. It includes any asset that will not become cash within 12 months, or is not a tangible asset used to provide service to patients and operate the practice. For example, ABC Medical Corporation may have a long-term deposit related to its building lease.

Long-Term Liabilities

Long-term liabilities represent any amounts not due to be paid for at least 12 months. The most common type of long-term liability is long-term financing from banks or other financial institutions.

Owners' Equity

Under the corporate form of business, the amount that owners contribute to the practice is generally called *owners' equity*, although it may be called *shareholders' equity* or *stockholders' equity*, among other titles. The owners' contributions may come in several forms. The first is the purchase of common stock. Common stock represents the actual ownership interest of the owners. It is usually the number of common shares owned that determines who has control of the corporation. Common stock can be either par or non-par. The designation of par or non-par is a legal issue and usually relates to state incorporation laws. Many states require corporations to maintain a minimum amount in owners' equity; this amount is related to the par value of the stock.

Par value is usually set relatively with $1, $10, or $100 being common. Some states do not have this designation. In our example, ABC Medical

Corporation is incorporated in a par-value state and has set the par value of its stock at $1. To raise enough capital, ABC Medical Corporation would have to sell quite a few shares at $1, or it could sell shares for an amount great than $1. ABC Medical Corporation chose the latter. It reports the amount received in excess of $1 per share when it sold its stock in the account called *additional paid-in capital.* Looking at ABC Medical Corporation's balance sheet, the reader of the financial statements knows that:

- ABC Medical Corporation is incorporated in a par-value state;

- Par value is $1; and

- ABC Medical Corporation issued 1,000 common shares at an average price of $94.97 ($1,000 par value plus $93,967 additional paid-in capital divided by 1,000).

Another term on the balance sheet related to ABC Medical Corporation's stock is *shares authorized.* Under the articles of incorporation of ABC Medical Corporation, 5,000 is the most shares that ABC Medical Corporation can issue. If ABC Medical Corporation would ever want to issue more than 5,000 shares, the common stock holders would have to vote to increase the number of authorized shares.

Another way that owners can invest in a corporation is through retained earnings. Retained earning are earnings the corporation has made in prior years, but not returned to the owners in the form of dividends. In many practices, earnings are retained to preserve cash for investments in new equipment and technology. Once the equipment has been purchased, the cash is gone. This is a key concept: Retained earnings do not represent a sum of cash available to the physician–owners. For ABC Medical Corporation, the physician–owners' total investment is the sum of the common stock, additional paid-in capital, and retained earnings, or $308,472. The readers of ABC Medical Corporation's balance sheet know that ABC Medical Corporation has total assets of $937,551 and of that amount, outsiders have a claim on those assets of $603,768. The remaining $308,472 is available to the physician–owners.

The Income Statement

While the balance sheet reflects a single point in time, the income statement covers a period of time (Figure 6.2). Notice that on ABC Medical Corporation's income statement the caption reads, "for the year ended Dec. 31, 2006." The income statement can be thought of in five parts:

- practice gross margin;

- physician expenses and operating income;

Figure 6.2   Anderson, Bailey, and Comstock Medical Corporation Income Statement—
for the Year Ended Dec. 31, 2006

Revenue		
Professional Receipts		$2,750,980
Total Revenue		2,750,980
Operating Expenses		
Personnel Expenses	$665,466	
Building and Equipment Maintenance	241,083	
Depreciation Expense	24,418	
Bad Debt Expense	37,550	
Building Rent	298,265	
General and Administrative	123,231	
Advertising	144,226	
Total Operating Expenses		1,534,239
Gross Margin		1,216,741
Physician Expenses		944,277
Net Operating Income		272,464
Other Income and Expenses		
Interest Expense	(42,714)	
Building Sublease	39,838	
Total Other Income and Expense		(2,876)
Net Income (Loss) Before Taxes		269,588
Taxes on Income		80,876
Net Income for Period		$188,712
Earnings per Share		$188.71

© 2007 Ann Gabriel

NOTE: This sample income statement appears in Appendix E on the CD so that you can use it as a template.

- non-operating income and expenses;
- income before income taxes and taxes on income; and
- net income and earnings per share.

Practice Gross Margin

This section of the income statement reports the revenue generated from serving patients, and the expenses incurred to provide those services. As stated previously, the income statement presents all the revenue earned during the period and all the expenses incurred to earn those revenues. For example, a doctor sees a patient on October 15 and addresses the patient's problem. On October 15, the doctor has earned all the revenue related to treating the patient. Similarly, if the doctor has nurses or physician's assistants who assisted, the doctor has incurred the expense of their salaries on October 15 as well. For most practices, personnel expenses are by far the largest expense. These expenses include both salary and benefits of professional clinical assistants as well as office staff. In general, personnel expenses do not include physician–owner salaries. Those salaries are usually included in a separate section of the income statement.

General and administrative could include expenses such as outside billing services, office supplies, utilities, and miscellaneous taxes not related to income.

The concept that the income statement should report all expenses incurred to generate the revenue earned is called the *matching principle*. It is because of the matching principle that we have the allowance for doubtful accounts, and the related bad debt expense. Given the practice's history, the accountant knows that not all of the revenue earned from treating patients will be collected. At the time the financial statements are prepared, the accountant does not know which one of the patients or insurance companies will not make the expected payment. But the accountant does know statistically that a certain percentage will not. Because the goal is to match all expenses incurred to the revenue generated, the accountant records bad debt expense on the income statement, and increases the allowance for doubtful accounts on the balance sheet. When the accountant determines who is not going to pay the amount due, he/she charges the account against the allowance for bad debt and not the income statement. Notice that cash is never expended for bad debt expense. Instead, bad debt expense represents cash not collected for services previously earned.

The accumulated depreciation and depreciation expense accounts are similar. Property and equipment are purchased with the intent to use them over a long period to generate revenue through patient services. Depreciation expense is an estimate of how much of the cost of the asset was used to generate revenue during the current period. Again, as similar to bad debt expense, there is no cash expended in relation to depreciation expense. Financing arrangements are made at the time that property and equipment are purchased. Cash is paid in accordance to the terms of the financing arrangements. Depreciation expense is not related to how the property or equipment is financed. Instead, it is an approximation of how the value of the property and equipment is diminished over time as they are used to generate revenue for the practice.

Gross margin represents the revenue generated through providing services to patients less the cost incurred to produce those services. It represents the amount available to compensate the physician–owners and cover other non-operating expenses of the practice.

Physician Expenses and Operating Income

Physician expenses can be a very broad category and can be defined at the discretion of the physician–owners. It generally includes the physicians' salaries, benefits, continuing education and memberships, and insurance costs. Operating income then becomes the gross margin less the physician expenses. It represents the income generated from operating the practice. This is the most important line on the income statement. The physician–owners presumably started the practice to serve their patients profitably. Operating income tells the physician–owners how well they are meeting that goal.

Non-Operating Income and Expenses

Some practices may have income or expenses not related to the practice per se. For example, ABC Medical Corporation has some excess space in the building it leases, and is subleasing that space until the practice expands and needs the space. ABC Medical Corporation is not in the business of leasing buildings, so the income from the sublease should not be a part of the operating income. It is income earned and, therefore, should be included on the income statement in the non-operating section. Financing expenses are also classified as non-operating. This is primarily to allow potential lenders or investors to make comparisons between two practices.

ABC Medical Corporation has taken out a loan with the local bank to finance its leasehold improvements. The interest on the loan is classified as a non-operating expense. The physician–owners of another practice could choose to increase their capital contribution to finance leasehold improvements. By classifying interest expense as a non-operating expense, it is easier for readers of the financial statement to make comparisons between the operations of competing practices.

Income Before Income Taxes and Taxes on Income

ABC Medical Corporation has elected to adopt a corporate legal structure and is, therefore, subject to corporate income taxes. As discussed in chapter 1 of Volume 1 (The Smarter Physician: Demystifying the Busines of Medicine in Your Practice, ©2007 MGMA), "Business Structures in Health Care," the tax treatment for other legal structures will vary.

Non-operating income and expenses are deducted to determine income before income taxes. Income before income taxes is generally considered the second most important line on the income statement after operating income. Because income taxes are considered to be outside the control of the physician–owners of the practice, income before income taxes provides an overview of how well the physician–owners have managed the practice. Income tax expense is calculated at statutory or legal rates, and includes all taxes on income. That is, state or local taxes as well as federal taxes are included in this line item.

Net Income and Earnings Per Share

Income tax expense is deducted from income before income taxes to arrive at net income. Notice that there are several lines with the title "Income," but there is only one "Net Income" on the income statement. This represents the net earnings of the practice for the period being reported on. Net income is also one of the items that links the balance sheets together. The retained earnings at the beginning of the period, plus net income for the period less any dividends paid to the owners, will equal the retained earnings at the end of the period.

The last item on the income statement is earnings per share. Remember that the common shares represent the ownership of the practice. One thousand common shares have been sold to the physician–owners of ABC Medical Corporation. A given physician–owner may own more or less shares than other physician–owners. Unlike general partnerships where each partner shares equally in the net income for the year, the number of shares owned determines how the net income of a corporation is to be shared by the owners. Earnings per share tell a physician–owner how much of the net income is attributed to his/her ownership.

Statement of Cash Flows

Like the income statement, the statement of cash flows (Figure 6.3) covers a period of time. Notice that on ABC Medical Corporation's statement of cash flows the caption reads, "for the year ended Dec. 31, 2006." The statement of cash flows can be thought of in three parts: operating activities, investing activities, and financing activities. These three sections are related to the three sections of the balance sheet and describe how cash was received or expended to cause changes in the balance sheet.

Operating Activities

Operating activities relate to changes in current assets and liabilities. The first line of this section is net income. It provides a second link between

Figure 6.3   Anderson, Bailey, and Comstock Medical Corporation Statement of Cash Flows—
for the Year Ended Dec. 31, 2006

Cash Flows from Operating Activities		
Net Income (Loss)		$188,712
Depreciation Expense	$24,418	
Accounts Receivable, Net	(28,395)	
Supplies	(2,754)	
Prepaids	(10,366)	
Accrued Expenses	(19,913)	
Taxes Payable	31,149	
Change in Current Assets and Liabilities		(5,861)
Net Cash Provided (Used) by Operating Activities		182,851
Cash Flows from Investing Activities		
Purchase of Computer Equipment	(11,832)	
Net Cash Provided (Used) by Investing Activities		(11,832)
Cash Flows from Financing Activities		
Increase in Notes Payable	75,000	
Notes Payable Repayment	(58,108)	
Net Cash Provided (Used) by Financing Activities		16,892
Net Increase in Cash		187,911
Cash at Beginning of Period		584
Cash at End of Period		$188,495

© 2007 Ann Gabriel

NOTE: This sample statement of cash flows appears in Appendix E on the CD so that you can use it as a template.

the balance sheet and the income statement. If all revenue earned and all expenses incurred were paid in cash, net income would also provide a link between cash at the beginning of the period and cash at the end of the period. However, cash is not always collected when revenue is earned and cash is not always paid when expenses are incurred. The rest of the operating activities section describes those differences.

Depreciation expense is added back to net income. Depreciation expense was subtracted on the income statement to arrive at net income, but it does not cause the expenditure of cash. Increases in current assets during the period use cash while decreases in current assets during the period provide cash. For example, when patient revenues are earned, accounts receivable increases and the patient revenue is included in net income. If the balance in accounts receivable increases during the period, it means that more patient revenue was recorded in net income than was received in cash. The increase in accounts receivable must be subtracted from net income to reflect the cash received from patients. Just as income from operations is the most important line on the income statement, cash provided by operating activities is the most important line on the statement of cash flows. Investors and lenders want the operations of the practice to generate sufficient cash to sustain the practice and pay long-term debts as they come due.

Investing Activities

Investing activities relate to changes in long-term assets. This would include both the purchase and the sale of property and equipment or other long-term assets. It is normal to see cash used by investing activities as a negative number on the cash flow statement. It is a positive indicator because it shows reinvestment in the practice. The practice is investing in new property and equipment to better serve patients and keep up with technology. If the practice is generating cash by selling property and equipment, it is usually in a dangerous situation.

Financing Activities

Financing activities relate to changes in long-term liabilities and owners' equity. It includes the acquisition of new debt as well as payment on new and existing debt. It also includes issuance of new shares of common stock, or payment of dividends to the physician–owners. It is not possible to determine whether cash provided by or used by financing activities is a positive or a negative indicator without further review. If the practice is taking on debt to finance new property and there is positive cash flow from operating activities, cash used by financing activities is a positive sign. It also indicates that the practice is investing to better serve patients and the operations of the practice are generating enough cash to cover the debt payments. If the practice is borrowing to cover day-to-day operations, cash provided by financing activities is an indicator that the practice may soon be facing financial difficulty.

The sum of the cash provided (used) by operating activities, investing activities, and financing activities is the net increase (or decrease) in cash for the period. Net increase (or decrease) in cash is the other item that links the balance sheets together. The net increase (or decrease) in cash, plus the cash at the beginning of the period, will agree with the cash at the end of the period.

Summary   Financial accounting identifies, measures, and communicates financial information to investors, creditors, suppliers, and other parties who do business with an economic entity. The information provided to these interested parties must be useful for investment and/or credit decisions. To serve this purpose, financial accounting must provide information that is both relevant to the decision to be made, and of sufficient accuracy to be reliable for decisionmaking purposes. In addition, because investors or creditors may have to make decisions between two entities, accounting information must also be comparable and consistent across all entities.

There are three basic financial statements that must be provided to users of the financial information. The balance sheet presents a picture of the entity at a specific point in time and reports the assets (or the resources the entity has to support its operations), which must equal the liabilities (or what it owes its suppliers and creditors), plus owners' equity (or what the owners have contributed to the entity and what is available for them).

The income statement and the statement of cash flows cover a period of time and provide the link between two balance sheets. The income statements present all the revenue earned during the period, and all the expenses incurred to earn those revenues. The net income for the period on the income statement is the link between the owners' equity on the period end balance sheet and the one for the previous period. On the other hand, the statement of cash flows tells the reader of the financial statements how cash was generated during the period and how it was spent. The net increase (decrease) in cash for the period is the link between the cash on the period end balance sheet and the one for the previous period.

Chapter 7

Using Financial Statements to Make Decisions

E. Ann Gabriel, PhD, CPA

As discussed in chapter 6, "Financial Statements: What They Are and What They Tell Us," financial accounting identifies, measures, and communicates financial information to investors, creditors, suppliers, and other parties who do business with an economic entity. But what type of information is needed and how is it useful in decisionmaking? This chapter will provide several examples and tools that can be used to conduct further analysis of financial statements and financial decisions.

Ratio Analysis

A useful tool for both investors and creditors is ratio analysis. Information necessary to perform ratio analysis can be found in the financial statement. It must be remembered that ratios in and of themselves are just numbers. It is important to compare ratios to the ratios of similar practices, historical ratios for the practice, or budgeted or expected ratios for the current year. The four main ratios are liquidity, activity, profitability, and coverage, and each has its benefits and uses (see Table 7.1).

Liquidity Ratios

Liquidity ratios are of most concern to suppliers and other short-term creditors. They measure the ability of the practice to pay its short-term obligations when they are due. The most common liquidity ratio is the current ratio, which is calculated as total current assets divided by total current liabilities. For Anderson, Bailey, and Comstock Medical Corporation (ABC Medical Corporation) whose financial statements appear in Figures 6.1, 6.2, and 6.3, the current ratio is $318,242 ÷ $185,274 = $1.72. ABC Medical Corporation expects to collect $1.72 for every $1 that it expects to expend during the next 12 months. A supplier would probably feel comfortable in extending credit to ABC Medical Corporation. However, some creditors may feel that drug and clinic supplies and pre-paids do not really generate cash and may want to exclude those

Table 7.1   Financial Ratios

Type of Ratio	Measures	Examples of Use
Liquidity	Short-term ability to pay maturing obligations	Current ratio Quick or acid ratio
Activity	Effectiveness in using assets employed	Receivables turnover Days outstanding Asset turnover
Profitability	Degree of success or failure for a given period	Return on assets Return on revenue Return on equity
Coverage	Degree of protection for long-term creditors and investors	Debt to total assets Debt to equity Times interest earned

©2007 Ann Gabriel

amounts from the calculation. They may instead use the quick ratio, which includes only cash and accounts receivable in the numerator. For ABC Medical Corporation, the quick ratio would be ($188,495 + $107,068) ÷ $185,273 = $1.60. Even excluding drug and clinic supplies and pre-paids, ABC Medical Corporation's expected cash receipts far exceed its expected cash disbursements.

Activity Ratios

The second type of ratios is activity ratios, which indicates how efficiently the practice is being run. It should always be the aim of the practice or of any business to collect cash as quickly as possible. This will allow the practice to pay debt quicker or to be able to avoid short-term credit. Two ratios can be used to provide information as to how efficiently patient receivables are being managed. The first is accounts receivable turnover, which is calculated as professional receipts divided by accounts receivable. It indicates how many times accounts receivable are collected during the period—the higher the turnover, the better. For ABC Medical Corporation, the accounts receivable turnover is $2,750,980 ÷ $107,068 = 25.7.

The second measure of activity is days outstanding. It is a measure of how many days it takes to collect from the patient or the insurance company once the revenue has been earned. Because it is best to collect cash as quickly as possible, the lower the days outstanding, the more efficient the practice is. To calculate days outstanding, the revenue per day is calculated as professional receipts ÷ 365. The result is divided into accounts receivable. For ABC Medical Corporation, the average professional receipt per day is

$2,750,980 ÷ 365 = \$7,537$. Days outstanding is then $\$107,068 ÷ \$7,536.93 = 14.20$. As a shortcut, days outstanding can also be calculated as $365 ÷$ accounts receivable turnover, which for ABC Medical Corporation would be $365 ÷ 25.7 = 14.20$. ABC Medical Corporation is able to collect from its patients or insurance companies in an average of 14.20 days. Whether that is good or bad depends on the average for similar practices and ABC Medical Corporation's historical average.

Businesses such as a medical practice with high investments in equipment may also find it useful to calculate the asset turnover. It is similar to accounts receivable turnover as it is calculated as professional receipts divided by total assets. Its interpretation is different, however. Asset turnover provides a measure of how well the practice uses its assets to generate patient services. ABC Medical Corporation's asset turnover is $\$2,750,980 ÷ \$937,551 = \$2.93$. This indicates that ABC Medical Corporation can generate $\$2.93$ of professional receipts for each $\$1$ it has invested in assets. Again, whether that is good or bad depends on the average for similar practices and ABC Medical Corporation's historical average.

Profitability Ratios

Profitability ratios provide a measure of how profitable the practice is. They usually are named *return on* and are calculated with net income in the numerator, and whatever the return is to be calculated on in the denominator. Some common return measures are:

Return on Assets = Net Income ÷ Total Assets

For ABC Medical Corporation the calculation is $\$188,712 ÷ \$937,551 = \$0.20$. This calculation says that ABC Medical Corporation was able to generate $\$0.20$ of net income for each $\$1$ it invested in assets.

Return on Revenue = Net Income ÷ Professional Receipts

For ABC Medical Corporation the calculation is $\$188,712 ÷ \$2,750,980 = \$0.07$. This calculation says that ABC Medical Corporation was able to generate $\$0.07$ of net income for each $\$1$ of professional receipts it generated. This is a very important profitability ratio. It indicates how much of the revenue is going to cover expenses, and how much is providing a profit to the physician–owners. It is very common to see growing revenues completely overtaken by growing expenses.

Return on Equity = Net Income ÷ Total Shareholders' Equity

For ABC Medical Corporation the calculation is $\$188,712 ÷ 308,472 = \$0.61$. This says that ABC Medical Corporation was able to generate $\$0.61$ for each $\$1$ invested by the physician–owners.

Coverage Ratios

Coverage ratios are of primary concern to long-term lenders to the practice. They are similar to liquidity ratios in that they provide evidence to lenders that the practice will be able to repay long-term debt when it comes due. The debt-to-assets ratio is calculated as notes payable minus current portion divided by total assets. It tells the lender what percentage of the practice's assets can be claimed by long-term lenders. For ABC Medical Corporation, the debt-to-assets ratio is ($443,806 − $90,118) ÷ $937,551 = $0.57. This says that $0.57 of every $1 of assets must be paid to long-term creditors in the future.

A second ratio of concern to long-term lenders is the debt-to-equity ratio, which is calculated as notes payable minus current portion divided by total owners' equity. This is a measure of how much of the practice's financing has been provided by physician–owners and how much has been provided by outside lenders. In general, lenders would prefer a lower ratio and physician–owners would prefer a higher ratio. In ABC Medical Corporation's case, the debt-to-equity ratio is ($443,806 − $90,118) ÷ $308,472 = $1.73. Outside lenders have provided $1.73 for each $1 provided by the physician–owners. As always, whether $1.73 is a positive or negative indicator depends on the ratio of other similar medical practices and ABC Medical Corporation's history.

The debt-to-assets and debt-to-equity ratios provide lenders with an indication of the practice's ability to repay debt in the long term. Lenders are also concerned whether they will be able to collect interest on a timely basis. For this reason, lenders are also interested in the times-interest-earned ratio, which is net income plus income tax expense plus interest expense divided by interest expense. It can also be calculated as operating income divided by interest expense. For ABC Medical Corporation, the times-interest-earned ratio is ($188,712 + $80,876 + $42,714) ÷ $42,714 = 7.3. ABC Medical Corporation generates enough income to pay its interest expense 7.3 times. Lenders would feel fairly certain that ABC Medical Corporation will be able to meet its interest payments and is more likely to be willing to lend to ABC Medical Corporation again in the future.

Depreciation

Recall from chapter 6 that property and equipment include the long-term tangible assets used to provide service to patients and operate the practice and are expected to be used to generate professional service revenue for many years. The cost of the property and equipment is charged against the income of the practice over its useful life. Depreciation expense is an estimate of how much of the cost of the asset was used to generate revenue during the current period. It is important to remember that no cash is expended in relation to depreciation expense. Financing arrangements are made at the time that property and equipment are purchased, and cash is paid in accordance with the terms of the financing arrangements. Depreciation expense is not related to how the property or equipment is financed. Instead, it is an approximation of how the value of the property and equipment is diminished over time as they are used to generate revenue for the practice.

There are several accepted methods for calculating depreciation. In choosing which method to use, several questions need to be answered:

- How much did the asset cost?

- What is the asset's useful life?

- What method is best for this asset?

Depreciation methods can be classified as either the tax depreciation method or financial accounting depreciation methods. Some medical practices use tax depreciation for preparing their financial statements. However, if they do so, they cannot say that their financial statements are in accordance with generally accepted accounting principals (GAAP) (see chapter 6 for a discussion of GAAP). Tax depreciation is governed by the modified accelerated cost recovery system (MACRS). The IRS has defined several classes of assets and how much depreciation can be taken on each class of asset each year. Most equipment common to medical practices will be in the five- or seven-year property classes.

Financial Accounting Depreciation Methods

Financial accounting depreciation is generally of two types: straight line or activity. For straight-line depreciation, the cost of the asset is depreciated ratably over its useful life. Under the activity method, the cost of the asset is depreciated each time it is used to generate patient revenue.

Each method can be used to analyze a purchase. Let's say that ABC Medical Corporation buys an ultrasound machine on Jan.1, 2002. The ultrasound machine costs $60,000 and has an estimated useful life of either 4 years or 3,000 ultrasounds.

Straight-Line Method

Using the straight-line method, the depreciation of the ultrasound machine per year would be found by the formula: $60,000 ÷ 4 = $15,000. (See Table 7.2.)

Table 7.2   Straight-Line Depreciation

Year	Book Value, Beginning of Year	Depreciation Expense	Accumulated Depreciation	Book Value, End of Year
2002	$60,000	$15,000	$15,000	$45,000
2003	$45,000	$15,000	$30,000	$30,000
2004	$30,000	$15,000	$45,000	$15,000
2005	$15,000	$15,000	$60,000	$0

©2007 Ann Gabriel

Notice that at the end of four years, the book value of the ultrasound machine is $0. This does not mean that the ultrasound machine is worthless. It just means that the all of the cost of the ultrasound machine has been charged against net income over the last four years. If ABC Medical Corporation sells the ultrasound machine after the four years, it will have to pay tax on the amount received.

Activity Method

Under the activity method, the cost of the asset is depreciated each time it is used to generate patient revenue, or $60,000 divided by 3,000 = $20 per ultrasound. (See Table 7.3.)

The number of ultrasounds performed per year during that period was:

- 880 in 2002;
- 780 in 2003;
- 900 in 2004; and
- 550 in 2005.

Notice that the book value of the ultrasound machine cannot go below $0. ABC Medical Corporation was able to perform a total of 3,110 ultrasounds with the machine instead of the 3,000 originally estimated over the four-year period. Taking the $20 per ultrasound times the 550 ultrasounds performed in 2005 would produce a depreciation expense of $11,000. However, the depreciation for the fourth year is only $8,800, or the book value, at the end of 2004. Again, the $0 book value at the end of 2005 does not mean that the ultrasound machine is worthless. It only means that the entire $60,000 cost of the ultrasound machine has been charged against net income over the four years.

Table 7.3   Activity Method Depreciation

Year	Book Value, Beginning of Year	Depreciation Expense	Accumulated Depreciation	Book Value, End of Year
2002	$60,000	$17,600	$17,600	$42,400
2003	$42,400	$15,600	$33,200	$26,800
2004	$26,800	$18,000	$51,200	$8,800
2005	$8,800	$8,800	$60,000	$0

©2007 Ann Gabriel

Table 7.4   Tax Depreciation Method

Year	Depreciation Rate	Book Value, Beginning of Year	Depreciation Expense	Accumulated Depreciation	Book Value, End of Year
2002	20.00%	$60,000	$12,000	$12,000	$48,000
2003	32.00%	$48,000	$19,200	$31,200	$28,800
2004	19.20%	$28,800	$11,520	$42,720	$17,280
2005	11.52%	$17,280	$6,912	$49,632	$10,368
2006	11.52%	$10,368	$6,912	$56,544	$3,456
2007	5.76%	$3,456	$3,456	$60,000	$0

©2007 Ann Gabriel

Tax Depreciation Method—MACRS

Under MACRS, the ultrasound machine would be classified as 5-year property even though its actual expected useful life is only 4 years. The IRS sets the depreciation rate for each year. If ABC Medical Corporation sold the ultrasound machine at the end of 2005, it would have a tax basis of $10,368. ABC Medical Corporation would not have to pay tax on the sale of the ultrasound machine unless it was sold for more than $10,368. (See Table 7.4.)

Capital Budgeting

As discussed previously, practices invest in property and equipment to serve patients and support operations of the practice. A key question to be answered before an investment is made is whether the investment is profitable in the long run. To answer this question, practices or their accountants complete a capital budget analysis. The term *capital budgeting* is used because most practices have several possible investments to choose from and limited funds to acquire them. The capital budgeting process helps determine which investments in property and equipment are the most profitable.

The key concept in the capital budgeting process is the time value of money or compound interest. Simply put, a dollar today is worth more than a dollar a year from today because the dollar today can be invested to earn interest. With compounding, interest is earned on interest, so the longer an amount is invested, the larger the sum gets. Suppose $1,000 can be invested for three years on Jan. 1, 2005, with an interest rate of 5 percent.

Balance 1/1/05	Interest Earned at 5%	Balance 1/1/05	Interest Earned at 5%	Balance 1/1/05	Interest Earned at 5%	Balance 1/1/05
$1,000	$50	$1,050	$52.50	$1,102.50	$55.12	$1,157.63

Notice that each year the interest earned increases as interest in year two is earned on interest earned in year one. Similarly, interest in year three is earned on interest earned in years one and two.

The five key components to the time value of money or compound interest are: present value, compounding period, interest rate, number of periods, and stream of payments.

Present Value

The first capital budgeting decision is whether one is interested in a present value or a future value. The example addresses a future value. One thousand dollars can be invested today and we want to know the amount in the account three years in the future. For physicians, most future value problems relate to personal issues. For example, you may want to know how much you will have saved for your children's college tuition or your retirement account, if you make deposits of a specified amount each month. Alternatively, you may want to know how much you need to deposit each month so that a desired amount will be available when needed for tuition or retirement.

Most business decisions are present value decisions. The practice will make an investment in property or equipment today to generate patient revenues in the future. Before making the investment, the physician–owners may want to know what the return will be on that investment. The process of calculating the present value of a stream of cash flows to be received some time in the future is also called *discounting*. (See Appendix F, Present Value and Future Value Tables.)

Table 7.5 Effect of Compounding Interest

Compounding Period	Effective Interest Rate	Amount at the End of Five Years
Annual	12%	$17,623.42
Semi-annual	6%	$17,908.48
Quarterly	3%	$18,061.11
Monthly	1%	$18,166.97

©2007 Ann Gabriel

Compounding Period

The compounding period sets the interval at which interest is added to the principal balance. The shorter the compounding period, the faster the balance grows. For example, assume that $10,000 can be invested for a period of 5 years. The annual rate of interest is 12 percent. The amount that will be in the account at the end of 5 years depends on the compounding period. (See Table 7.5.)

Interest Rate

The interest rate is the percentage that will be paid on the principal balance at the end of the compounding period and it consists of three elements; the risk-free rate, inflation risk, and credit risk. The risk-free rate is the rate that would be charged if the lender were positive that the debt would be repaid. It is often set at the rate of U.S. Treasury Bills. Inflation risk provides a buffer for changes in interest rates in the future—the longer the investment term, the higher the inflation risk element. That is why interest rates on 30-year mortgages are usually higher than rates on 15-year mortgages. The final element is the credit risk element and relates to the specific credit risk the borrower poses to the lender. This is why it is so important for consumers to know what is in their credit files, and to understand their credit ratings. Credit ratings apply to businesses as well as individuals; a practice would have a credit rating separate from the physician–owners. While interest rates are always quoted in annual terms, interest rates must be adjusted to match the compounding periods. As in the example, a 12-percent annual interest rate would be 6 percent if the compounding period is semi-annually, 3 percent if it is quarterly, or 1 percent if it is monthly.

Number of Periods

The number of periods must match the compounding period. In the example, there are 5 periods when the compounding period is annual,

10 when it is semi-annual, 20 when it is quarterly, and 60 when it is monthly.

Stream of Payments

The final element is the stream of payments. Payments may occur once (single sum) or as a series of like payments (annuity). Most business transactions for investments in property and equipment require monthly payments of like sum.

In the capital budgeting process, the expenditure of cash today to acquire property or equipment is compared to the present value of the inflow of cash generated through the use of the property or equipment in the future. The expenditure of cash today includes more than the purchase price of the property or equipment. For example, the cash expenditure can include cash expended for purchase price, delivery, installation, and testing of equipment, cash expended for hiring and training people to operate equipment, cash expended for supplies or inventory, and cash inflows for tax credits available or sale of existing equipment.

Future cash inflows come from two main sources:

- **Operating cash flows.** Operating cash flows may be generated because of either increased revenues or cost savings. To calculate operating cash inflows, the cash expended to provide patient services is subtracted from the revenue generated. For example, the salary and benefits of the nurse or physician's assistant who performs an ultra-sound would be subtracted from the revenue generated by providing the ultrasound. For simplicity, projected income statements are often used as proxies for operating cash flow with adjustment for major items such as depreciation; and

- **Terminal cash flows.** Terminal cash flows result when the property or equipment is sold at the end of its useful life. This is an important consideration and is often overlooked. The terminal cash flow may make the difference in the decision to invest in a certain piece of property or equipment or to forego the investment. Terminal cash flows include cash inflow from the sale of the equipment, net of taxes.

Assessing Investment Choices

When there are several investment choices, how can physician–owners decide which investments to make? Three common methods used to make investment choices are payback period, net present value (NPV), and internal rate of return (IRR).

Figure 7.1   Net Present Value (NPV) Method

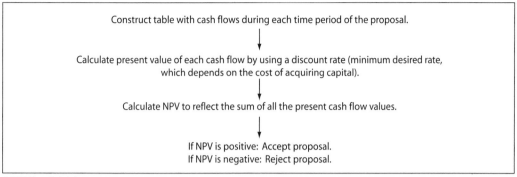

Construct table with cash flows during each time period of the proposal.

Calculate present value of each cash flow by using a discount rate (minimum desired rate, which depends on the cost of acquiring capital).

Calculate NPV to reflect the sum of all the present cash flow values.

If NPV is positive: Accept proposal.
If NPV is negative: Reject proposal.

Payback Period

The payback period is concerned only with how long it takes to recover the cash outlay.

Net Present Value

Under this method, the present value of all cash outflows discounted at an appropriate interest rate is subtracted from the sum of the present value of all cash inflows discounted at the same interest rate. A positive number indicates that the present value of the net cash inflows to be received in the future from providing patient services is greater than the cash expended today to acquire the property or equipment. The higher the result, the better it is. (See Figure 7.1.)

Internal Rate of Return

Under this method, the interest rate at which the present value of the cash inflows equals the present value of the cash outflows is calculated. That interest rate can then be compared to interest rates available to the practice.

A key question in both the NPV and IRR methods is what interest rate to use in the calculations. As a minimum, the practice would want to cover any cost of borrowing, plus provide for a return. For example, if the practice could borrow from the local bank at a 10 percent rate of interest, the practice might use 12 percent to 16 percent in the calculations to cover the interest expense and provide a return on the investment. Practices will also build in extra cushion to cover contingencies. (See Figure 7.2.)

Figure 7.2   Internal Rate of Return (IRR) Method

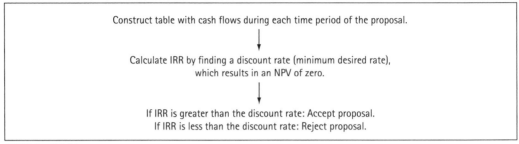

© 2007 Ann Gabriel

NOTE: The discount rate that one picks depends on what the best alternative investment of similar risk will yield to the investor.

Investment
Decision-
making
at Work

Suppose ABC Medical Corporation wants to expand its outpatient clinic and provide additional laboratory services. The cash outlay to acquire the laboratory equipment, including installation of the equipment and training the staff, is $150,000. ABC Medical Corporation's accountant has estimated that the net additional cash inflow will be $40,000 per year.

Should ABC Medical Corporation invest in the additional equipment and provide the laboratory services? The following paragraphs show how ABC uses the methods explained in this chapter to make a decision.

If ABC Medical Corporation considers the payback method, the cash outflow to acquire the laboratory equipment will be recovered in 3.75 years. That is, it will take about 80 percent of the useful life of the equipment to recover the cash outflow. Whether this is acceptable to ABC Medical Corporation depends on the experience of similar medical practices and other investment options it might have.

ABC Medical Corporation can also consider the investment's NPV (see Figure 7.1), or the IRR (see Figure 7.2). NPV problems are most easily addressed using spreadsheet packages. ABC Medical Corporation's accountant has determined that the cost of capital (that is, the cost of borrowing, plus the cushion mentioned before) is 12 percent. ABC Medical Corporation would want a return of 12 percent before it would invest in the additional laboratory equipment.

Considering only the $40,000 net cash inflow to be generated each year, the NPV of the investment is negative $5,186.56. The IRR is 10 percent. Because the NPV is negative and ABC Medical Corporation wants a return of at least 12 percent, it would not want to invest in the laboratory equipment and provide the additional laboratory services. However, there may be other information ABC Medical Corporation would need to take into consideration before a final decision is made. For example, it may be necessary for ABC Medical Corporation to provide the additional laboratory services to remain competitive in its market.

There is another item of information that ABC Medical Corporation has not considered in this scenario. ABC Medical Corporation has not considered any cash inflow (net of taxes) that can be generated by selling the equipment at the end of 5 years. Suppose that ABC Medical Corporation's accountant estimates that the laboratory equipment can be sold for a net cash inflow of $15,000. That changes the answer considerably. As these calculations show (see Figure 7.3), assuming the laboratory equipment can be sold, the NPV becomes $3,324.84 and the IRR is 13 percent. Now the investment in the laboratory equipment looks good. The NPV is positive and the IRR exceeds the minimum required. This is why it is important to consider all cash inflows and outflows when making decisions regarding long-term investments.

Selecting Financing

The final decision to be made in the capital budgeting process is how to finance the investment. Notice that this is a separate decision from the decision to acquire the property or equipment. The most common methods of financing are long-term borrowing and leasing. ABC Medical Corporation has the choice of buying the equipment or leasing it. If ABC Medical Corporation chooses to buy the equipment, it can obtain a loan from the local bank at a rate of 10 percent. The local bank will require a down payment when the laboratory equipment is purchased and annual payments thereafter. ABC Medical Corporation has also negotiated with a leasing company, which will finance the equipment for a fixed monthly payment for 60 months. At the end of the 60 months, ownership of the equipment will be transferred to ABC Medical Corporation.

Which financing option should ABC Medical Corporation choose? The answer again depends on the present value of the cash outflows. Because ABC Medical Corporation will only have cash outflows, the present value will be negative. The decision becomes which financing option has the least negative present value. ABC Medical Corporation has several down payment and payment options from which it can choose and still borrow at 10 percent (Figure 7.4). ABC Medical Corporation's decision depends on whether it has cash available for the larger down payment, or whether it wants to preserve cash now and have larger payments in the future.

Notice that a specific interest rate is not mentioned with the leasing option. This is common as the interest rate is hidden in the quoted

Figure 7.3   Outpatient Center—Cost of Capital

Purchase lab equipment at cost	$150,000.00
Estimated increased net cash inflow per year	40,000.00
Estimated life of lab equipment, in years	5.00
Cost of capital	0.12

Scenario 1

Assume lab equipment will be outdated at the end of 5 years, so cannot sell

		Net Cash Out	Pay-Back Period	Net Present Value	Internal Rate of Return
Yr 0	($150,000.00)			($5,186.56)	10%
Yr 1	40,000.00	($110,000.00)			
Yr 2	40,000.00	(70,000.00)			
Yr 3	40,000.00	(30,000.00)			
Yr 4	40,000.00	10,000.00	3.75 yrs		
Yr 5	40,000.00	50,000.00			

Scenario 2

Assume same scenario but can sell at the end of 5 years and receive $10,000 after taxes

		Net Cash Out	Pay-Back Period	Net Present Value	Internal Rate of Return
Yr 0	($150,000.00)			($5,186.56)	10%
Yr 1	40,000.00	($110,000.00)			
Yr 2	40,000.00	(70,000.00)			
Yr 3	40,000.00	(30,000.00)			
Yr 4	40,000.00	10,000.00	3.75 yrs		
Yr 5	40,000.00	50,000.00			

One-Time Payment

Yr 5	$15,000.00			$8,511.40	
Total Net Present Value				**$3,324.84**	**13%**

© 2007 Ann Gabriel

NOTE: This sample spreadsheet appears in Appendix E on the CD so that you can use it as a template.

payments. For purposes of the present value calculation, ABC Medical Corporation will use the 10-percent interest rate quoted by the local bank. If the lessor is willing to accept payments less than $3,188 per month for 60 months, leasing would be the better option. If the payment

Figure 7.4   Outpatient Center—Cost of Leasing

Purchase lab equipment at cost		$150,000.00	
Estimated life of equipment, in years		5.00	
Buy		**Lease**	
Put $50,000 down and pay $26,380 per year for 5 years		Pay $2,300 per month for 60 months	
Interest rate: 10%			
		Net Present Value	Net Present Value
	Total	($149,997.33)	($150,044.40)
Yr 0	($50,000.00)	Month	
Yr 1	(26,380.00)	1	(3,187.00)	(3,188.00)
Yr 2	(26,380.00)	2	(3,187.00)	(3,188.00)
Yr 3	(26,380.00)	3	(3,187.00)	(3,188.00)
Yr 4	(26,380.00)	4	(3,187.00)	(3,188.00)
Yr 5	(26,380.00)	5	(3,187.00)	(3,188.00)
		6	(3,187.00)	(3,188.00)
		7	(3,187.00)	(3,188.00)
		8	(3,187.00)	(3,188.00)
	Net Present Value	9	(3,187.00)	(3,188.00)
	($150,000.95)	10	(3,187.00)	(3,188.00)
		11	(3,187.00)	(3,188.00)
		12	(3,187.00)	(3,188.00)
		13	(3,187.00)	(3,188.00)
		14	(3,187.00)	(3,188.00)
Buy		15	(3,187.00)	(3,188.00)
Put $25,000 down and pay $32,975 per year for 5 years		16	(3,187.00)	(3,188.00)
Interest rate 10%		17	(3,187.00)	(3,188.00)
		18	(3,187.00)	(3,188.00)
	Total	19	(3,187.00)	(3,188.00)
Yr 0	($25,000.00)	20	(3,187.00)	(3,188.00)
Yr 1	(32,975.00)	21	(3,187.00)	(3,188.00)
Yr 2	(32,975.00)	22	(3,187.00)	(3,188.00)
Yr 3	(32,975.00)	23	(3,187.00)	(3,188.00)
Yr 4	(32,975.00)	24	(3,187.00)	(3,188.00)
Yr 5	(32,975.00)	25	(3,187.00)	(3,188.00)
		26	(3,187.00)	(3,188.00)
		27	(3,187.00)	(3,188.00)
	Net PresentValue	28	(3,187.00)	(3,188.00)
	($150,001.19)	29	(3,187.00)	(3,188.00)
		30	(3,187.00)	(3,188.00)
		31	(3,187.00)	(3,188.00)
		32	(3,187.00)	(3,188.00)
		33	(3,187.00)	(3,188.00)
		34	(3,187.00)	(3,188.00)

(Figure continued on next page)

Figure 7.4   Outpatient Center—Cost of Leasing (continued)

		Net Present Value	Net Present Value
Buy	35	(3,187.00)	(3,188.00)
Put $15,000 down and pay $27,000 per year for 5 years	36	(3,187.00)	(3,188.00)
Plus interest at 10%	37	(3,187.00)	(3,188.00)
	38	(3,187.00)	(3,188.00)
Total	39	(3,187.00)	(3,188.00)
Yr 0 ($15,000.00)	40	(3,187.00)	(3,188.00)
Yr 1 (35,613.00)	41	(3,187.00)	(3,188.00)
Yr 2 (35,613.00)	42	(3,187.00)	(3,188.00)
Yr 3 (35,613.00)	43	(3,187.00)	(3,188.00)
Yr 4 (35,613.00)	44	(3,187.00)	(3,188.00)
Yr 5 (35,613.00)	45	(3,187.00)	(3,188.00)
	46	(3,187.00)	(3,188.00)
	47	(3,187.00)	(3,188.00)
	48	(3,187.00)	(3,188.00)
Net Present Value	49	(3,187.00)	(3,188.00)
($150,001.29)	50	(3,187.00)	(3,188.00)
	51	(3,187.00)	(3,188.00)
	52	(3,187.00)	(3,188.00)
	53	(3,187.00)	(3,188.00)
	54	(3,187.00)	(3,188.00)
	55	(3,187.00)	(3,188.00)
	56	(3,187.00)	(3,188.00)
	57	(3,187.00)	(3,188.00)
	58	(3,187.00)	(3,188.00)
	59	(3,187.00)	(3,188.00)
	60	(3,187.00)	(3,188.00)

NOTE: This sample spreadsheet appears in Appendix E on the CD so that you can use it as a template.

required by the lessor is greater than $3,187, ABC Medical Corporation should choose to buy the equipment.

Summary   Financial accounting is to financial statements what clinical applications are to basic science research. The knowledge gained in understanding financial statements is applied in this chapter for the reader to make everyday decisions in the form of ratio analysis, depreciation, capital budgeting, and calculation of the best investment choices.

Chapter 8

Measuring Profit and Loss: The Roles of Cost and Volume Measurements

Medical practice managers need to arrive at costs for different services in order to manage expenses better, set charges based on realistic numbers, bid for contracts, and, most important, do a profitability analysis for a service or procedure. While a detailed explanation of cost accounting is beyond the scope of this chapter, it is helpful to understand how to classify various costs. Once cost is understood, a very important progression is to use cost for an analysis of profit using volume of services. The most useful concepts for most physician-related activities are discussed here.

Types of Cost

Although we often use the terms *cost* and *expense* interchangeably, in an accounting sense, a cost is an amount spent to purchase an asset (such as dollars spent on purchasing an ultrasound machine). Expense is an amount spent to use an asset, such as dollars spent on staff, supplies, utilities, and so forth, to provide the ultrasound service. In any case, cost is classified in several ways depending on the purpose of determining cost. Those purposes include: volume, traceability, management, and accounting.

Volume

When measured based on volume (Table 8.1), costs can be measured in terms of whether they are fixed, variable, or semi-variable (also known as step costs). In summary:

- **Fixed costs** do not fluctuate with volume of services or products. Office rent, utilities, and equipment lease expenses generally are fixed expenses. They generally will not vary with the number of patients seen in the office;

- **Variable costs** fluctuate proportionately with volume of services and products. Supplies such as dressings, immunization injections, or

Table 8.1   Average Cost in Relation to Volume

Number of Tests	Fixed Costs	Variable Costs	Fixed and Variable Costs	Cost per Test (average)
0	$20,000	$0	$20,000	$0
10	20,000	50	20,050	2,005.00
50	20,000	100	20,100	402.00
100	20,000	125	20,125	201.25
200	20,000	175	20,175	100.88
500	20,000	300	20,300	40.60
750	20,000	375	20,375	27.17
1,000	20,000	450	20,450	20.45
1,500	20,000	575	20,575	13.72
2,000	20,000	675	20,675	10.34

©2007 Satiani

NOTE: This table appears in Appendix E on the CD so that you can use it as a template.

disposable examination gowns are variable costs. The expense will vary with the volume of supplies used; and

- **Semi-variable** or **step costs** change incrementally as volume changes. If a physician sees 100 more patients a week, it is reasonable to assume that he/she will incrementally see an increase in the phone bill. Although the basic charges may be fixed, the additional phone calls make this a semi-variable cost.

Traceability

The traceability purpose of accounting looks at costs differently. This viewpoint categorizes costs as either direct or indirect:

- **Direct costs** are those that can be traced to a specific object such as a department, division, service, or product. Many of the major expenses in a physician's office, such as employee salaries and supplies, are examples of direct costs; and

- **Indirect costs**, or **overhead expenses**, are those that cannot be directly traced to a specific object such as a department, division, service, or product. The benefits paid to employees, administrative expenses, equipment maintenance, and housekeeping expenses are examples of indirect costs.

Even though most physician office managers find it easier to assign benefits as an indirect expense, a better way to approach this is to break down employee benefits individually, assign them to each employee, and classify the benefits as a direct cost.

Costs of non-revenue producing departments in hospitals, such as administration and accounting, are allocated to various revenue-producing departments by several methods. The most common is the step-down method. This detail may not be necessary in an office setting, but is necessary in a large health care facility.

Management

When tracking cost by its management purpose, the two major categories to consider are:

- **Operating costs:** those linked with the output of a service or product; and

- **Non-operating costs:** those costs that support the function for producing a service or product.

Accounting

In what is called managerial accounting, information on sub-units, such as divisions or departments, is used for internal management decisions. Financial accounting, on the other hand, captures all the economic activities of the organization for investors or other outside interested parties.

Other Types of Costs

Sunk costs are those already incurred in any project. Therefore, they are not necessarily a factor in future decisionmaking. An example is when your practice decides to cut its Saturday morning office hours. Perhaps you had renovated or added on to your facility in some way to accommodate these extra hours. The cost of any construction, depreciation, insurance expenses, and salaries already paid for that renovation are examples of sunk costs, which will have no bearing on future projections. In other words, you've already spent that money. Most sunk costs are fixed costs, but not always.

Opportunity costs measure the cost of a missed opportunity and the benefits that could have been received from that opportunity. Unfortunately, the true cost of a project is often not obvious, unless one considers the value of the resources spent on the best alternative. As an example: a tenant in the office building you own moves out and you must decide whether to hire an additional physician and expand your practice into that space, or sign up another tenant to rent the space. Before you make any projections on the profit or loss of the additional practitioner and related costs, it is important to ask: what is the opportunity cost or value (rental income) that you will lose by not renting the space to someone else?

Differential costs are those that express the difference in costs between two parallel courses of action.

Avoidable costs are those that can be eliminated if the service or procedure is ended. Both fixed and some variable costs can be avoidable, if certain activities are eliminated.

Incremental cost is the opposite of avoidable cost. These are costs incurred with an increase in volume of that particular service. For example, if a practice is already performing 1,000 tests, an additional contract with an insurance company that generates 250 more tests will generate incremental cost. Up to a certain point, the variable cost for the 1,000 tests may be enough to cover the additional volume, but at some point additional cost will be incurred.

Using Cost–Volume–Profit Analysis

Cost–volume–profit (CVP) analysis[1,2] is a method used to gauge the consequences of changes in a company's volume of activity on costs, revenue, and profits. Profit is revenue minus expenses. Profits may be a function of many factors including: volume, price, fixed cost, variable cost, and the payer mix. As previously mentioned, fixed costs are related to a time period rather than variation in volume; variable costs change proportionally with an increase or decrease in volume.

Contribution margin—a term commonly used in break-even analysis—is simply the difference between the total sales revenue and the variable costs assigned to it. In other words, contribution margin is what remains from revenues to cover fixed costs when all variable costs are covered.

As shown in Figure 8.1, when we look at costs incurred over a certain period of time (a month, quarter, or annually), fixed costs stay constant and variable costs change depending on the volume of services. The break-even point is when the volume is such that total expenses are equal to revenues and, therefore, the organization breaks even without any profit or loss. As indicated in Figure 8.1, the break-even point is at the intersection of the total cost and total revenue lines. The logical next step is to gauge whether the volume necessary to reach the break-even point can be achieved by the price set for the service or procedure. The CVP analysis allows the manager or physician to then change assumptions (volume or price) repeatedly and observe the effect on profit.

Figure 8.1   Cost–Volume–Profit Concept

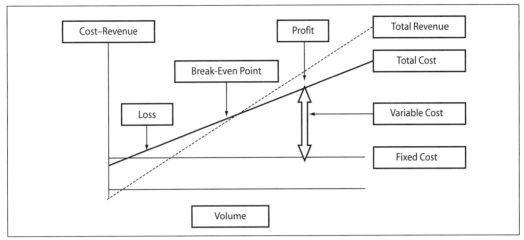

© 2007 Satiani

Sensitivity analysis or a "what-if?" analysis can also be used to arrive at how profitability changes with a change in one of many variables such as volume.

On-line calculators can also be used to ascertain break-even points provided the following values are known: fixed cost, variable unit cost, price, total variable cost, total revenue, and expected unit sales.[3] The term *unit* means a unit of measure of the amount of service delivered. This can be a single level of patient encounter or a lab test.

The following calculations are handy to use in figuring the break-even point:

- Contribution margin per unit equals sales price per unit minus variable costs per unit;

- Contribution margin ratio equals contribution margin per unit divided by sales price per unit; and

- Break-even sales volume equals fixed costs divided by the contribution margin ratio.

Examples   **Introducing a New Laboratory Test**

You are considering introducing a new laboratory test for your patients with a one-time equipment cost of $20,000 (fixed cost), as shown in

Table 8.1. You know that the cost of supplies, reagents, and maintenance will increase with unit usage (variable cost). You also know that the average cost per test (total cost divided by the number of tests) will decrease as the volume increases. The next step is to project a realistic number of tests that will be performed and find the break-even point.

An Office Purchase

You are considering purchasing a new ultrasound machine that has a fixed cost of $100,000, generates revenue of $500 per test, and variable costs associated with testing of $50.

One way to analyze this scenario is to understand how many tests need to be performed in order for you to cover your initial $100,000 investment. If you had $0 costs associated with each test, you would divide your initial investment by $500, the revenue you receive from each test. However, your cost for performing the test is $50. This results in your actually earning $450, or $500 minus $50, per test. Dividing $100,000 by $450 yields a break-even point of 222.22, or 223, tests. After performing 223 tests, each test (which generates $450) becomes pure profit because you no longer have to pay off your equipment.

In this example, you calculated your *contribution margin* without even realizing it. We did this by subtracting $50 from $500. This term refers to what portion of your revenue can be used to cover your fixed expenses. In this case, our fixed expenses are the $100,000 investment.

The contribution margin percentage is 9 percent, which is the charge ($500) minus the variable cost. This is reached by dividing the variable cost ($50) by the charge ($500).

The break-even point in dollars is $111,111, which can be found by dividing the contribution margin percentage (0.90) by the fixed cost ($100,000). In other words, $111,111 of revenue is the point at which all fixed costs have been covered and any subsequent revenue from additional tests is a profit.

Hospital Room Charges

A small rural hospital (100 beds) charges $500 for a semi-private room. The accounting department has calculated that variable expenses (nursing, food, linen, etc.) are $300 per patient and that the hospital's fixed expenses are $1 million annually. The board has set a goal to reach a $3-million annual profit.

Therefore, the administrator must run the following calculations:

Contribution margin per bed

Bed Charge ($500) – Variable Expense per Patient ($300) = $200

Break-even point in volume

Fixed Expense ($1 million) ÷ Contribution Margin
per Bed ($200) = 5,000 Bed Days

Break-even point in dollars

Break-even Point in Volume (5,000 Bed Days) × Bed
Charge per Day ($500) = $2.5 million

Contribution margin ratio

Contribution Margin per Bed ($200) ÷ Bed Charge ($500) = 0.40

For the hospital to cover its $1-million annual expense, and also reach its target of a $3-million annual profit, it must actually generate $4 million.

Bed days to reach profit target

Fixed Expense ($1 million) + Profit Target ($3 million) ÷ Contribution
Margin per Bed ($200) = 20,000 Bed Days

Therefore, if the hospital has 100 beds open daily, it has a potential occupancy of 36,500 beds, or bed days, annually. Based on our calculation, it must have 20,000 occupied bed days to reach its goal. This means that the hospital must have an occupancy rate of 54.79 percent. You can calculate this amount by dividing 20,000 bed days by the 36,500 potential bed days available.

In-Office Procedure

Suppose a physician is charging $375 for an office procedure and wants to find out exactly:

a. What it costs to do the procedure;

b. What the break-even point is in terms of volume (the number of procedures) and dollars; and

c. How much revenues would increase if the charge for the procedure was increased to $400 (assuming the market will support that charge).

To solve (a), let us assume that the manager adds up all the resources used (variable costs) and assigns a final cost to a single procedure ($23.90) as shown in Table 8.2. Then, all annual fixed costs, including physician and staff salaries, benefits, and other fixed costs (Table 8.3) are added ($202,463).

Table 8.2   Variable Costs of Supplies by Unit, Item, Treatment

| Supplies | Variable | | | | |
	Number in Unit	Cost/Unit ($)	Cost/Item ($)	Number of Items Used in a Treatment	Cost per Treatment ($)
Syringes	100	9.64	0.10	6.00	0.58
Solution (mL)	30	32	1.07	12.00	12.80
Cotton balls	4,000	10.55	0.00	40.00	0.11
Needles	100	28	0.28	6.00	1.68
Tape (rolls)	12	6	0.50	0.33	0.17
Band-aids	100	3.88	0.04	15.00	0.58
Scalpels	10	3.87	0.39	1.00	0.39
Gauze	100	4.73	0.05	4.00	0.19
Gloves	100	3.93	0.04	6.00	0.24
Paper gowns	100	84	0.84	2.00	1.68
Chucks	300	35	0.12	3.00	0.35
Towel	500	12.44	0.02	2.00	0.05
Stopcock	50	83.5	1.67	1.00	1.67
Linen				2.00	1.00
Appointment cards	500	72	0.14	3.00	0.43
Printing costs					1.00
Digital pictures					1.00
Total					23.90

©2007 Satiani

NOTE: This table appears in Appendix E on the CD so that you can use it as a template.

Table 8.3   Fixed Costs for In-Office Procedure

Fixed Annual Costs	Total ($)
Staff salaries	79,576
Staff benefits	19,894
Other overhead assigned	102,993
Total fixed cost	202,463

©2007 Satiani

NOTE: This table appears in Appendix E on the CD so that you can use it as a template.

Table 8.4   Total Variable and Average Costs per Office Procedure

		CVP Analysis		
Volume	Fixed Costs ($)	Total Variable Cost per Procedure ($23.90)	Total Cost ($)	Average Cost per Procedure ($)
0	202,463	23.90	202,486.90	0
100	202,463	2,390	204,853	2,048.53
200	202,463	4,780	207,243	1,036.22
300	202,463	7,170	209,633	698.78
400	202,463	9,560	212,023	530.06
500	202,463	11,950	214,413	428.83
622	202,463	14,865	217,328	349.40
700	202,463	16,730	219,193	313.13
800	202,463	19,120	221,583	276.98
900	202,463	21,510	223,973	248.86
1,000	202,463	23,900	226,363	226.36

©2007 Satiani

NOTE: This table appears in Appendix E on the CD so that you can use it as a template.

To solve (b), we can use the calculation steps demonstrated in the previous examples. The contribution margin per procedure is equal to $375 minus $23.90, or $351.10. The break-even point in number of procedures is equal to $202,463 ÷ (375 − 23.90), or $576.65. We will round this up to $577. The break-even point in total dollars is equal to $202,463 ÷ 0.94, or $215,386.

The latter amount is what is needed to pay all the annual salaries, benefits, and expenses related to providing the procedures.

If the charge per procedure is increased to $400, the break-even point in procedures would be $202,463 ÷ (400 − 23.90) or 538 procedures (Table 8.4).

References

1. W.O. Cleverley, and A.E. Cameron, *Cost Concepts and Decision Making: Essentials of Health Care Finance,* 5th ed. Gaithersburg, MD: Aspen Publishers (2002): 227–251.

2. L.C. Gapenski, *Managerial Accounting: Healthcare Finance,* 2nd ed. Chicago: Health Administration Press (2001): 129–164.

3. KJE Computer Solutions LLC, "Financial Calculators," http://dinkytown.com/java/BreakEven.html (accessed July 23, 2006).

Part 3

Physician Compensation

Chapter 9

Models, Methods, and Philosophies

Physician compensation methods have continued to evolve with the advent of managed care and other changes in health care. Compensation based purely on ownership and the volume of work performed in a fee-for-service era has evolved into a payment system based on a mix of capitation, limited utilization models, and employment in a managed care system.

The basic difference between private practice and full-time employment within a hospital, government agency, or a university is that of ownership vs. employment. Physicians choosing ownership fear that working in a health care system or other large organization would result in a loss of autonomy in patient care, loss of incentive to work harder, and a bureaucratic structure. Increasingly, full-time employment within health care systems and universities has meant more job security and minimal interference in patient care practices. In return, for some loss of autonomy and differences in salary between private practice and, for example, academic practice, non-cash benefits and other advantages are offered instead.

There is no single method for compensating physicians within a group, a hospital, university, or health care entity that is acceptable for all concerned. Each circumstance is different. The health care market and the demand and supply in each specialty determine the compensation. An ideal method is one that allows for the greatest productivity from a satisfied physician who delivers the best quality of care. Productivity is defined as "the individual physician's charges net of adjustments for contractual allowances or collections."[1]

Rather than just focusing on the annual salary, it is imperative that physicians, especially those starting their first job, look at the entire compensation package, including salary, benefits, retirement plans, vacation, and any incentives. Various professional organizations and consulting firms publish salary and productivity data based on surveys of physicians,

Table 9.1   Sources for Physician Salary Information

Organization	Contact	Fees (2006)	Information Based on
Medical Group Management Association (MGMA)	www.mgma.com 800.275.6462, ext. 1888	$280 for members, $330 for non-affiliates, $495 for non-members	44,781 medical practices/ providers
Merritt Hawkins & Associates	www.merritthawkins.com 469.524.1400	Free	Income offers made in 2,840 national-recruiting assignments in 15 specialties
American Medical Group Association (AMGA)	www.amga.com 612.376.9530	$225 for members, $450 for non-members	Salary and productivity data from 35,000 member physicians in 199 specialties
Cejka Search	www.cejkasearch.com 314.726.1603	$150 for American College of Physician Executives, $350 for non-members	Permanent placements made by consulting activities
Hay Group	www.haygroup.com 215.861.2319		Survey of 15,722 physicians in 112 specialties and 114 organizations
Jackson & Coker	www.jcnationwide.com 866.284.3328, ext. 5554		Survey of 2,541 physicians in 18 specialties
Modern Healthcare	www.modernhealthcare.com 888.446.1422 subscription	Free for subscribers of magazine/Website	Multiple surveys published in July each year
Faculty Practice Solutions Center (FPSC)	www.facultypractice.org 630.954.4717		Data from such areas as physician productivity, financial, and operational management collected by University HealthSystems Consortium and Association of American Medical Colleges (UHC-AAMC)
Association of American Medical Colleges (AAMC)	www.aamc.org 202.828.0975	$70 for members, $120 for non-members (not-for-profit); $170 for non-members (for-profit)	

groups, and institutions (Table 9.1). Although these benchmarks are helpful, there are multiple factors that influence physician compensation: value to the hiring entity, geography, existing patient base of physicians moving between practices locally, competitiveness with other similar practices in the area, unique clinical or academic skills, reputation, and finally, comparison with accepted published benchmarks.

Compensation Methods

Compensation methods start with the traditional fee-for-service or discounted fee-for-service method. This straightforward method takes the gross revenue collected by a physician, minus all the direct (insurances, educational expenses, benefits) and indirect costs, and the balance is paid to the physician. No allowance is made for other non-clinical responsibilities. With the increasing complexity of the health care system, many variations of this basic plan now exist. Physicians respond well to plans based on:

- **Fairness.** The compensation should be based on some objective measures. If part of the compensation is based on performance, then regular reviews should be performed with a chance for the physician to see and respond to the review;

- **Transparency.** The method for determining salary and particularly bonuses should be disclosed to the entire group. Well-defined standards should be agreed upon that include the past two years performance and comparison with external benchmarks in the same specialty; and

- **Incentives.** Physicians are by nature competitive and most prefer some productivity measure as part of a compensation package.

Elements of a Compensation Plan

Compensation methods are as varied as the needs of physicians and the entities hiring them. The three essential elements of a compensation plan are base salary, bonuses or incentives, and benefits. The hardest part is structuring incentives in a way that is fair and minimizes "gaming" of the system. The easy part is measuring the patient or clinical work performed. This can be done by measuring specific factors, as discussed in the following sections.

Gross Charges and Collections

Gross charges may reflect how much work was performed, but actual revenue collected is a more important measure of value to the practice. Another way to get at a net cash position for each physician is to deduct his/her share of practice expenses from the revenue collected.

For example, Physician A's actual revenue collected is $250,000. Subtracted from this amount is $85,000 in operating expenses, which includes $70,000 for a share of the practice's fixed costs (staffing, facility rent, etc.), and $15,000 for a share of variable costs (supplies, etc.). The result is $165,000 in compensation.

Sharing of this information with the physician group, along with a side-by-side comparison of their peers, tends to generate competitive behavior.

A disadvantage is that unless adjustment is made for low-paying tasks or caring of sicker patients, there may be no incentive for anyone to do essential tasks that do not generate significant income.

Relative Value Units

In an era of stable charges, and payment by third-party payers and patients based on billed charges, gross (or net) charges were an adequate measure of productivity. However, because of significant variances due to managed care, relative value units (RVUs) are now an essential part of any financial assessment of individual physician performance. As indicated in a previous chapter, about 50 percent of the RVU component is work RVUs (WRVUs), while the rest is made up of the practice expense and the malpractice expense. For example, if a Level 3 office visit (CPT® code 99213) is worth 1.41 RVUs, the WRVU is 0.67, and the balance (0.74 RVU) is for practice and malpractice expenses.

It has always been difficult to measure productivity due to large variances in what different insurers would pay for the same service. The use of RVUs levels the playing field in terms of variations in fee schedules, complexity of work, and a high percent of Medicaid patients. It also basically eliminates the need to use gross or net charges as a productivity measure. With this measure, physicians within a group who have more uninsured patients, or a high percentage of Medicaid patients, are thus fairly evaluated for the amount of work performed, even though they may collect less revenue.

On the other hand, a practice is not paid in RVUs. Ultimately, productivity from a cash standpoint is measured by how much revenue the physician collects. RVUs do provide an answer to the question: "How hard am I working relative to others in the group and nationally?" The method also rewards physicians who record patient visits and services accurately and code to the legitimate highest reimbursement level allowed. National benchmarks are available from organizations such as MGMA and the FPSC. FPSC is an entity formed by UHC-AAMC that gathers data on academic physician productivity, and on operational and management functions.

A variation of calculating bonuses based on RVUs is to use the same percent as the individual RVU production used to calculate salary, and apply that to any profit remaining at the end of the year. As an example, assume that Physician A of a 5-member group produced 30 percent of the group's RVUs for the year, and the salary was distributed accordingly. Let us assume the group has $60,000 left over at the end of the year as a profit, and the group is looking at an equitable way to distribute the profit. Physician A then would receive 30 percent of the profit ($18,000) as an incentive bonus.

Non-Clinical Productivity (Intangibles)

The second part of a compensation plan is the non-clinical contribution to the practice. Intangibles such as the reputation that results in referrals to the group, expertise in a field, or the influence of the individual within the hospital that may result in favorable treatment of the entire group by hospital administration, are examples of added value that is not easily captured with RVUs or collection numbers. In the academic environment, it is particularly important to capture the individual's contribution to research, teaching, publishing, and outreach lectures. These have to be considered in any formula for compensation. It may be worthwhile to have group members come up with a list of intangibles they consider important and assign a score to each task (Table 9.2). Some of these are:

- Research;

- Teaching;

- Administrative role (such as medical directorship) that increases the influence of the group within the hospital or health system;

- Outreach activities (lectures, conferences that increase visibility of the group);

- Publications that raise the profile of the group locally and nationally;

- Committee participation that results in added influence with the hospital and medical staff;

- Patient satisfaction scores, if available;

- Outcomes data; and

- Credit for travel time for satellite clinics. This can be calculated by assigning WRVUs to the travel time.

If, for example, the group pays all of its physicians a base salary equal to 50 percent of each physician's total compensation, then another 35 percent may be determined by productivity, and the rest (15 percent) may be determined by the factors just mentioned. If all compensation is being paid based either entirely on productivity, a fixed salary, or a combination of both, the group may choose to select the intangibles important to them. Then they

Table 9.2   Sample Non-Clinical Activity Scoring

	RVU	Credit Number	Total RVUs		RVU	Credit Number	Total RVUs
Lectures/Presentations				**Civic Organizations**			
Invited lectures, visiting professor	2.0			Examples: Rotary, Kiwanis	1.0		
				Civic awards	1.0		
Paper presentation	2.0			**Research Activities**			
Outreach lecture	0.5			Grants from government, foundations, industry, NEW	2.0		
Conference/symposium organizer	3.0			Resident/student advisor	1.0		
Member/fellow in competitive organization	3.0			Grants from government, foundations, industry, RENEWAL	2.0		
Poster presentation	0.5			First author for grant, extra	1.0		
State/Regional				**Professional Organizations**			
Society officer/council/ study section	0.5			Member in peer-reviewed organization	2.0		
Boards/commissions	1.0			President/officer	3.0		
Publications				Committee member/ council/task force	2.0		
Peer review article (1st/last author)	3.0			**Education**			
Peer review article (middle author)	2.0			**Conference attendance**			
Book chapter	1.0			>50%	1.0		
Book editor	3.0			Staff meeting, department, section	0.5		
Journal editor/board	3.0			**Medical education meeting**	0.5		
Media mention, paper, radio, television	1.0			Small group lecture (new)	0.8		
Committees				Small group lecture (repeat)	0.6		
Officer/chair committee	2.0			Large group lecture (new)	1.0		
Admissions/curriculum	2.0			Large group lecture (repeat)	0.8		
Medical staff leadership position	2.0			Non-clinical one-to-one teaching	1.0		
Medical staff committees, task force, ad-hoc	1.0			**Outcomes**			
Department chair/vice chair	4.0			Mortality and outcome measures equal or better than national benchmarks	4.0		
Division chief	4.0			**Patient Satisfaction Awards**			
Program director	2.0			Patient letter with kudos	1.0		
Task force/ad hoc committee	2.0			Patient complaint letter	−1.0		

NOTE: This table appears in Appendix E on the CD so that you can use it as a template.

Table 9.3   Sample Compensation Based on Clinical and Non-Clinical RVUs

	Physician A	Percent of Group	Compensation ($40 per RVU)
RVUs			
Clinical	12,744	17%	509,760
RVUs Intangibles			
Teaching	300		12,000
Research	100		4,000
Outreach	325		13,000
Publications	75		3,000
Outcomes	150		6,000
Civic	50		2,000
Total			549,760
Overhead expenses		17%	256,000
Individual expenses			28,000
Total expenses			284,00
Total compensation			265,760

NOTE: This table appears in Appendix E on the CD so that you can use it as a template.

could assign them a weight, and phase them in over a period of time to allow everyone to adjust and gravitate toward areas in line with their strengths.

Because non-clinical activities cannot be directly measured in RVUs, proxy RVUs have to be created to allow such contributions to be recognized.[2] As indicated in Table 9.3, all activities can be converted into RVUs, and multiplied by the volume to give the total RVUs.

As an example:

- Peer-reviewed article, first author, equals 3.0 RVUs;

- Task force or ad hoc committee membership equals 2.0 RVUs; and

- Small group lecture equals 0.8 RVUs.

The payment for the intangibles can be paid annually or semi-annually as a bonus once the activities have been confirmed, collated, and dollar amounts assigned. Some disadvantages include: the record-keeping involved; the system measures quantity of work not quality; potential gaming of the system may be possible; some activities may not be easily measurable; and the unlikelihood that all physicians will be on board with the RVU value assigned to each activity.

Three Common Revenue Distribution Methods

The trend in physician groups in practice has been to move away from fairly complicated formulas to one of three basic methods discussed here.

Fixed Salary Minus Expenses

In the compensation method based on fixed salary minus expenses, the physician receives a fixed salary and splits income and bonuses equally with associates after deducting all expenses. The method does reduce utilization because there is no incentive to perform extra services or tests. The method is simple, easily understood, and allows for a predictable budget for the organization. While the utilization for the health care system is possibly reduced, productivity also declines.

Productivity Minus Expenses

In this compensation method based on productivity minus expenses, income is based entirely on productivity, which can be measured by RVUs, collections, or a similar target, minus the expenses. The expenses are a combination of allocation of general overhead, plus individual expenses such as automobile allowance, meeting expenses, and so forth. For a new associate, the group may elect to split any revenues with the new physician if his/her production exceeds the salary, and after all expenses have been covered. For instance, if the associate has been guaranteed $200,000 in salary and his/her production not only covers salary and expenses (overhead), but generates another $100,000 in revenue, the group may elect to split the excess 50/50 as an incentive for the new physician to work harder.

Salary Plus Productivity

A salary plus productivity compensation plan includes some combination of a base salary and productivity-based compensation. An example based on an excellent step-by-step method by Wenzel and Wenzel is shown in Table 9.4.[3] There are arguments for and against a fixed salary regardless of productivity. This arrangement has the advantage of simplicity, easy record-keeping, discouraging intergroup competition, and maintenance of a group culture. However, it is likely that some members of such a group may not be as productive as others and simply coast, leading to hidden hostility among the high producers that eventually leads to

Table 9.4 Hypothetical Scenario: Year-End Bonus Calculated Based on Compensation (70% equal share and 30% productivity)

	Assumptions*	Physician A	Physician B	Physician C	Physician D	Physician E	Physician F	Total	Comments
RVUs, $		12,744	11,291	13,458	12,841	13,725	10,157	74,216	
RVUs, as percent of group		17	15	18	17	18	14	100	
Charges, $		1,326,541	1,157,875	1,520,503	1,386,785	1,414,335	1,043,408	7,849,447	
Payments, $		475,991	402,878	692,067	492,405	494,845	404,443	2,962,629	1,790,730 (70% of 2,962,629)
Gross collection, percent		36%	35%	46%	36%	35%	39%	38%	767,456 (30% of 2,962,629)
Expenses, total, $		450,000	385,000	360,000	405,000	380,000	380,000	2,360,000	1,652,000 (70% of 2,360,000)
Receipts shared 70%, $	70% of 2,962,629/6 physicians	345,640	345,640	345,640	345,640	345,640	345,640	2,073,840	708,000 (30% of 2,360,000)
30% of receipts split by productivity (RVUs), $		152,618	135,218	161,669	153,780	164,367	121,637	888,789	
Total allocated compensation, $		498,258	480,858	506,809	499,420	510,007	466,277	2,962,629	
Expenses, split equally, $	70% equally, fixed	275,333	275,333	275,333	275,333	275,333	275,333	1,652,000	
30% of expenses split by productivity (RVUs), $	30% based on RVUs	121,574	107,713	128,386	122,500	130,933	96,895	708,000	
Overhead expenses, $		396,908	383,046	403,719	397,833	406,266	372,228	2,360,000	
Individual expenses, $		28,000	26,000	30,050	33,000	29,500	31,000	177,550	
Total expenses, $		424,908	409,046	433,769	430,833	435,766	403,228	2,537,550	
Total bonus after expenses, $		73,351	71,811	73,040	68,587	74,241	64,049	425,079	

* Expenses include regular salary paid to physicians. Revenues shared 70% equally, 30% productivity. Expenses shared 70% equally, 30% based on RVUs productivity.

NOTE: This table appears in Appendix E on the CD so that you can use it as a template.

tension and eventual breakup of the group. Designing incentives involves making some difficult decisions and getting a buy-in from all stakeholders within a group. The incentives must be large enough to generate interest. Any plan with less than 20 percent of the physician's compensation at risk does not create enough motivation.

Monitoring Production

Tables 9.5 and 9.6 show the data needed to monitor physician productions with a medical group. These include:

Total revenue of the group and per physician member. Production as demonstrated by gross charges, patient encounters, and RVUs is monitored. If a compensation plan is based heavily on RVUs, accurate coding

Table 9.5   Sample Format of Typical Financial Summary of a Practice

Item	Current Year	Prior Year	Percent Change from Previous Year
Gross charges			
Net receipts			
Gross collections			
Net revenue			
Expenses, operating/administrative			
Expenses, physician-related			
Net income			
Accounts receivable in days			
Other Measures			
WRVUs per physician			
Revenue per WRVU			
Cost per WRVU			
Days cash on hand			
Operating margin			
Debt-to-capital ratio			
Payer mix			
Medicare			
Medicaid			
Top five insurers			
Payment by payer			
Medicare			
Medicaid			
Top 5 payers			

NOTE: This table appears in Appendix E on the CD so that you can use it as a template.

Table 9.6   Sample Format of Summary of Accounts Receivable

Month	Charges	Payments	Adjustments	Beginning A/R	Ending A/R	Collection %
January						
February						
March						
April						
May						
June						
July						
August						
September						
October						
November						
December						
Year						
Previous Year 1						
Previous Year 2						
Previous Year 3						
Previous Year 4						
Previous Year 5						
Previous Year 6						

NOTE: This table appears in Appendix E on the CD so that you can use it as a template.

and capture of all patient contact must be enforced. It is useful for all physicians to see their RVUs on a rolling basis for the past 12 months and compared to members of the group and to national benchmarks for the same specialty.

Total overhead expenses (administrative and clinical) of the group and individual expenses. In a recent survey, 51 percent of physicians admitted to overhead costs of 51 percent or greater; 26 percent said their overhead costs exceeded 61 percent of revenue; and a small percent (1.4 percent) stated the overhead exceeded their revenues.[4] Almost a third surveyed said they would not be able, or doubted they will be able to support their overhead.

Monitoring of accounts receivables. This is illustrated in Table 9.6.

All data recorded for each physician by RVU. These data will include total and individual production, total and individual revenue, and overhead expenses. There are some activities such as executive physicals or cosmetic procedures that are not recognized by the RVU system adopted by the Health Care Financing Administration—the predecessor to the Centers for Medicare and Medicaid Services. There is a way to convert this service into RVUs in order to have a uniform way to track productivity. For example, if a cosmetic hair removal procedure is paid $120 and a Level 2 visit is charged $80, the ratio is 1.5:1. To convert the cosmetic service, the RVU for the office visit (1.1) is multiplied by 1.5 to come up with 1.65 as the RVU for the hair removal service.

Payer mix. This can simply be a breakdown of the practice's major payers by the gross charges received from each. The mix can be divided by payer type (private, Medicare, Medicaid, workers' comp, self-insured, other). Alternately, the measurement could be by RVUs or other measurements. Payer mix changes with the demographics and contractual arrangements and must be monitored at least yearly.

Performance measures. As mentioned previously, a database of all the intangibles or the non-revenue producing needs to be maintained. (Table 9.2).

Production in Academic Practices

Comparison of individual production with well-known benchmarks such as those published by the MGMA, AMGA, and AAMC for academic practices is extremely valuable. For physicians who are just starting practice, these benchmarks are an excellent source of comparative data with the caveat that it may take 12 months to 24 months until a new member generates reliable and consistent productivity numbers.

As an example, let us assume there are 6 full-time equivalent (FTE) faculty members in the Department of Neurosurgery. Also assume that the academic medical center (AMC) calculates that each faculty member is spending 75 percent of his/her time on clinical services for a total of 4.75 CFTEs (clinical FTEs) for the entire department. The next steps in benchmarking involve:

1. Comparing individual and group compensation with the median compensation for other academic or private practices;

2. Comparing median gross charges, collections, and WRVUs individually and for the group with other academic and private practice groups; and

3. Adjusting the numbers for the fact that faculty are not classified as 6 FTEs but 4.75 CFTEs.

Although compensation for academic faculty has traditionally not been based upon clinical production, there is increasing pressure to generate clinical revenue similar to private practices.

Compensation in Academic Practices

For academic practices, although practice revenue has become a major source of compensation, support from the university/medical school is required to keep recruiting competitive with private practice. A faculty practice plan assumes a very important role for fulfilling the three major missions of the AMC—health care services, medical research, and education. Academic practice plans frequently look to national benchmarks of compensation (Tables 9.7, 9.8 and 9.9) in order to remain competitive in recruiting and retaining faculty.

Table 9.7   Medical School Full-Time Faculty Compensation (MD or equivalent degree), Total Compensation in thousand $, 2004–2005

	Instructor		Assistant Professor		Professor		Chairperson	
	Mean	Median	Mean	Median	Mean	Median	Mean	Median
Family practice	131	121	138	135	171	171	253	242
General internal medicine	132	125	137	131	194	183	325	264
General pediatrics	110	104	129	122	190	179	308	308
Pulmonary medicine	99	97	143	135	199	189	348	322
Nephrology	111	101	142	138	206	199	323	297
Gastroenterology	148	129	199	180	233	221	345	309
Hematology/oncology	120	109	156	143	229	214	354	350
Psychiatry	118	121	138	133	194	181	305	296
Cardiology	151	125	213	194	263	242	417	423
Radiology, diagnostic	198	175	271	261	310	306	458	440
Pathology, clinical	128	124	151	149	228	215	346	322
General surgery	129	91	219	205	308	284	525	496
Orthopedic surgery	192	149	306	280	355	337	533	452
Urology	87	62	225	204	302	300	434	392
Obstetrics/gynecology, general	145	150	196	182	281	249	361	341
Emergency medicine	170	175	185	182	220	212	328	311

Table 9.8   Compensation Survey for Physicians

	Merritt Hawkins & Associates, 2004–2005	MGMA 2005 Survey (2004 data)			Hay Group		Jackson & Coker	
	Mean salary to Recruits ($)	Median Amounts ($)	MGMA ($)	AMGA ($)	Hay Group ($)	Cejka ($)	Jackson & Coker ($)	Mean ($)
Family practice			173,409	190,000	158,700	171,700	142,200	167,202
General internal medicine			188,464	192,000	161,200	177,400	167,000	177,213
Pediatrics			177,631	195,000	161,600	167,700	155,600	171,506
Gastroenterology	298,000	368,733						333,367
Cardiology, non-invasive	320,000	351,637	393,138	410,000	307,800	386,600	325,000	364,508
Orthopedics	361,000	383,697	456,669	n/a	367,200	375,000	296,200	373,767
Ophthalmology	n/a	280,353						280,353
Psychiatry	n/a	180,000	198,016	201,000	180,000	186,000	178,000	188,603
Radiology, diagnostic	355,000	399,195	443,301	413,000	366,400	472,500	330,100	405,060
Anesthesiology	303,000	321,686	357,625	342,000	305,600	453,000	309,950	353,635
Surgery, general	220,000	282,504	325,968	336,000	249,700	252,000	250,200	282,774
Urology			375,502	378,000	267,300	288,000	279,200	317,600
Obstetrics/gynecology	247,000	247,348	277,521	292,000	219,000	232,900	237,350	251,754
Emergency medicine	n/a	221,679	245,579	248,000	208,400	180,000	219,000	220,196

Merritt Hawkins: Compensation figures based on income offers in national recruiting offers in 15 specialties in April 2006.

MGMA: Compensation figures are for 2005 and based on 44,781 providers nationwide, members and non-members.

AMGA: Compensation figures from 35,000 members in 199 specialties based on 2005 data.

Cejka: Compensation figures from 2005 based on permanent placements of 194 physicians in 16 specialties.

HAY Group: Compensation figures from 2005 based on salary survey of 15,722 physicians in 68 specialties.

Jackson & Coker: Compensation figures from 2006 based on survey of 2,541 physicians in 18 specialties.

Source: Reprinted with permission from *Modern Healthcare*, 36 (28) (2006): 28–30.

Usual Organization of Faculty Practice Plans

Regulatory restrictions in the form of anti-kickback statutes and Stark Laws require complicated arrangements between a tax-exempt practice plan and the teaching hospital. The physician faculty may be employed by the faculty practice plan (through a limited liability company or by a department), and the university. Most practice plans have been set up as tax exempt, and to receive support from the academic medical center, are set up to operate at a deficit. Under the Stark Laws, the AMC exception alone is not enough to allow all the complex arrangements between faculty, practice plan, and the medical center. Therefore, the "indirect compensation" exception is utilized to allow bonuses for clinical performance

Table 9.9 Recent Offers Made to New Resident Graduates, 2005

	Low ($)	High ($)	Average ($)
Internal medicine	130,000	250,000	162,000
Family practice	115,000	220,000	145,000
Psychiatry	130,000	230,000	174,000
Radiology	240,000	500,000	351,000
Orthopedics	250,000	515,000	370,000
Cardiology	175,000	500,000	342,000
General surgery	150,000	350,000	272,000
Urology	250,000	375,000	320,000
Obstetrics/gynecology	175,000	450,000	234,000
Gastroenterologist	175,000	500,000	315,000
Emergency medicine	130,000	270,000	230,000
Anesthesiology	275,000	375,000	306,000

The 2006 Review is based on 2,840 physician and certified registered nurse anesthetist (CRNA) search and consulting assignments Merritt, Hawkins & Associates® represented from April 1, 2005 to March 31, 2006.

Source: Reprinted with permission of Merritt, Hawkins & Associates, 2007.

and academic achievement. Under regulations issued in 2004, the Department of Health and Human Services acknowledged that there are many variants of an AMC. Provided a faculty practice plan is part of a bona fide AMC, and it supports the core teaching mission, it eliminates the requirement that the practice plan be organized in any particular manner. This presumably does away with the necessity of being a nonprofit, tax-exempt organization.[5]

Under the indirect compensation exception to the Stark Laws, the arrangement between the faculty, plan, and the academic medical center is not illegal provided the faculty compensation is at fair market value (which can be reflected in survey data by MGMA, AAMC, and AMGA), and is not based on the volume or value of the referrals from the physician to the center. Bonuses, if structured correctly, can be based not only on productivity, but also on the criteria previously mentioned, such as teaching and research contributions.

Most practice plans have a governing board that includes the dean of the medical school (either as chair or ex-officio), all department chairs, and possibly members-at-large from the community. Billing and collections can be centralized or decentralized and delegated to the departments with reporting to the board. All departments pay a certain percentage of their revenue to the dean (academic enrichment or dean's fund) to fund new programs, recruit new faculty, and subsidize non-productive departments and basic sciences. The percentage varies. Because it may be a disincentive to clinical faculty, a flat tax has been levied in some institutions. Physician compensation and any incentive plans are usually determined by the individual departments with the approval of the dean.

Special Issues for Physician Executives

Physicians are now increasingly gaining more experience in the management side of health care by further formal education. Organizations such as the American College of Physician Executives (ACPE), American College of Healthcare Executives, and MGMA are attracting more physicians as members. These organizations provide the learning necessary to lead hospitals, health care systems, managed care organizations, pharmaceutical companies, and large physician groups. The physician executive position in these organizations may be part time or full time. It may be an elected position within a medical staff structure or within a formal hospital administrative structure.

An elected voluntary position such as medical staff president has become a paid position because of its time demands. Several years ago, these positions were honorary positions and did not demand as much time as they do now. Most physicians in elected voluntary positions have a clinical practice, and the stipend for the voluntary position is fixed, with no benefits or retirement benefits. The individual and the group can then negotiate who gets to keep all or part of the stipend depending on the clinical load carried by the physician. This can vary as a percentage (from zero to 100 percent) of the stipend going to the physician depending on the clinical and call load, and any decrease in clinical activities due to the heavy time commitments of the position. The part-time position can pay anywhere from $10,000 to $80,000 annually, depending on the size of the medical staff and the hours involved. Department chairs (in non-academic institutions) are paid anywhere from $5,000 to $25,000 a year, again depending on the size of the department and the time commitment.

The position of vice-president of medical affairs is a full-time position within the administrative structure of the hospital and generally reports directly to the chief executive officer (CEO) of the hospital. It has become a very important role from both the medical staff and hospital administration perspective.

Table 9.10   Salary Ranges for Physician Executives

Position	Average Compensation (2005)	Source
Chief Medical Officer, Health Care Systems	$432,200	*Modern Healthcare,* www.modernhealthcare.com
Chief Medical Officer, Hospitals	$289,300	*Modern Healthcare,* www.modernhealthcare.com
Chief Medical Officer	$265,750	Cejka/ACPE Compensation Survey, 2005
Vice-President, Medical Affairs	$243,000	Cejka/ACPE Compensation Survey, 2005
Vice-President, Quality	$270,000	Cejka/ACPE Compensation Survey, 2005
Physician Advisor	$191,000	Cejka/ACPE Compensation Survey, 2005
Physician Executive Compensation, Urban	$259,994	MGMA Management Compensation Survey, 2006 Report
Physician Executive Compensation, Rural	Mean: $236,010 Median: $220,000 75th Percentile: $269,500	Cejka/ACPE Compensation Survey, 2005
Medical Director, full-time	$220,546	MGMA Management Compensation Survey, 2006 Report
Full-time Department Head/ Manager/Division Chair of Hospital	$280,000	Cejka/ACPE Compensation Survey, 2005

Source: Reprinted with permission from: *Modern Healthcare,* Medical Group Management Association; Cejka Search; and American College of Physician Executives.

The vice-president of medical affairs is the primary liaison of the hospital with all divisions of the medical staff including the medical executive committee, medical education, service line strategies, utilization, quality of care, and contract negotiations. The salary can range from a part-time salary of $125,000 upward to a full-time average salary of $243,000 (Table 9.10).

Other positions in the administrative structures of hospitals, large health systems, and even some very large medical groups are CEO, chief operating officer, and medical director of a division or a specialized section. A part-time medical director position is the most common position occupied by physicians within the hospital or health system. The medical director is almost always appointed by hospital or health system administration in consultation with physician leadership. The director serves to act as a liaison in his/her specialty with other physicians and the hospital or health system administration to ensure optimum functioning of the specialty area. The medical director reports either to the vice-president of medical affairs, or the CEO of the hospital or health system. Under the

Stark Laws, all compensation for physicians who are independent contractors (see chapter 19 in Volume 1 [The Smarter Physician: Demystifying the Business of Medicine in Your Practice, ©MGMA, 2007] regarding the Stark Laws) must be fixed in advance, and payment must not be based on a percentage of collections within a section or department supervised by the physician. For institutions accepting medical education funding from the federal government, accurate time-keeping on a monthly/quarterly basis by the physician and the hospital is mandatory.

Benefits as Part of a Compensation Package

There are several other important factors to consider in an employment package in addition to the rate of compensation (see chapter 8 in Volume 1, "Understanding and Negotiating the Physician Employment Agreement," for more details). These include fringe benefits such as:

Vacation. Paid time off work will vary depending on the time in practice, the duration with the group, specialty, and size of the group. In general, a physician starting practice with a group should expect paid vacation time of three to four weeks.

Sick time. Most small- to medium-sized groups do not have a specific number of sick days off as most physicians rarely take time off for illness. In larger groups or institutions, physicians are lumped in with all employees, and a schedule including accrual of sick days and additional personal days is specified.

Disability insurance. As mentioned in chapter 8 in Volume 1, long-term group disability policies are standard and are in relation to gross pay.

Life insurance. Term life insurance is also a standard benefit in most physician groups and unless a large amount of insurance is chosen, no medical evidence of insurability is necessary. The amount of coverage is usually 2.5 to 3 times the annual salary up to a maximum ceiling set by the insurer and the employer. The IRS may consider as taxable the value of benefits over $50,000 and employers may offer a waiver if the physician declines benefits over this amount. Some plans offer a small policy for dependents as well. Additional coverage (voluntary group term) may be obtained from the insurer at a personal cost, which is not deductible to the professional corporation.

Health insurance. Comprehensive health insurance with most of the premium paid by the corporation is a standard benefit. The coverage is similar to that offered to other employees, and usually includes dependent coverage. Most groups now have employees (including physicians) pay part of the health insurance premium.

Flexible spending account. This benefit is covered in detail in chapter 2, which discusses employee health insurance.

Retirement benefits. If the physician is fully employed by the hospital or health system, retirement benefits are in line with those for the top executives and tend to be very generous. Medical staff positions, part-time director jobs, and consulting-type roles do not come with retirement benefits. For physicians employed in a group practice, there may be a vesting period (generally one year); that is, physicians cannot transfer the corporation dollars deposited in the retirement plan elsewhere until employed for a specified period of time. See chapter 5 in Volume 3 (The Smarter Physician: Investing in Your Personal Financial Health, ©MGMA, 2007) for a more comprehensive discussion of retirement topics

Miscellaneous. Continuing medical education (CME) is granted by most groups separately or as a block of time with vacation time. Some groups allot a dollar amount ($1,000 to $5,000) per year that can be used for CME activities. Dues for professional organizations, subscriptions for journals, and parking fees for hospitals might also be paid by the employer. Highly recruited physicians might be able to negotiate additional fringe benefits such as car leases, help with educational loans, and other inducements; however, those benefits may bring tax consequences as their value is figured as part of compensation for income tax purposes.

Summary

Most private and academic practices are trending toward individual physician accountability by direct cost allocation methods. Measurement of net collections and WRVUs are most frequently used to reward productivity.

References

1. C.W. Hunter and M. Reiboldt, *Physician Compensation Strategies,* 2nd ed. Chicago: AMA Press (2004).

2. D.R. Willis, and others, "An Incentive Compensation System that Rewards Individual and Corporate Productivity," *Family Medicine* 36 (4) (2004): 270–278.

3. F.J. Wenzel and J.M. Wenzel, *Fundamentals of Physician Practice Management.* Chicago: Health Administration Press (2005).

4. P. Moore. "What's in Your Wallet?" *Physicians Practice* 16 (7) (2006): 23–35.

5. Department of Health and Human Services, "Rules and Regulations, Part III." *Federal Register* 69, No. 59 (March 26, 2004).

Chapter 10

Pay for Performance: A Work in Progress

The pay-for-performance concept is borrowed from the advertising industry, where advertisers bid to rank high in searches of the World Wide Web conducted on search engines such as Yahoo® or Google.™ The auction model, which has worked effectively as a pay-per-click system in advertising, aims to make health care more responsive by tying payment to certain specified measures related to quality, safety, patient satisfaction, and access to health care.

With the retirement of baby boomers, the growth of Medicare as a percentage of gross domestic product (GDP) is projected to increase the share of Medicare from 2.7 percent to almost 10 percent of GDP in the United States[1] (see Figure 10.1). Budgetary pressures may force Congress to try extraordinary measures to reduce this growth. Because the federal government is the largest payer, the Centers for Medicare and Medicaid Services (CMS), through the Medicare Payment Advisory Commission (MedPAC), has recently acted to support this concept and, as expected, private carriers have followed. Quality criteria from the Health Plan Employer Data and Information Set, also known as HEDIS, or the Consumer Assessment of Health Plans, are used as a benchmark.

Quasi-governmental organizations such as the Institute of Medicine (IOM) are rightly demanding a major initiative to improve the quality of care, and there is a confluence of events pushing the quality of care as a means for cost cutting to the fore. The IOM's report, "Performance Measurement: Accelerating Improvement" recommended that the federal government create an independent National Quality Coordination Board.[2] This board would exist within the U.S. Department of Health and Human Services (HHS), be chaired by a presidential appointee, and consist of members representing all constituencies. The board would lead the effort to study existing and new indicators of quality, create and maintain performance measures, and report findings to the public.

Figure 10.1   U.S. Health Expenditures on Health Services/Supplies as a Percentage of Gross Domestic Product (2005)

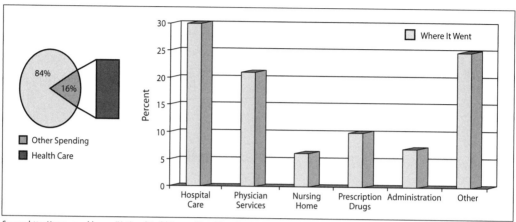

Source: http://www.cms.hhs.gov/NationalHealthExpendData/downloads/PieChartSourcesExpenditures2005.pdf.

NOTE: Figure also appears as Appendix G on the CD.

As part of the Medicare Prescription Drug, Improvement and Modernization Act (MMA) of 2003, Congress acted to create an incentive for hospitals to participate in the public reporting of quality information. Congress also penalized hospitals that did not report on 10 measures of quality by mandating a 0.4 percent reduction in their annual Medicare payment update for inpatient hospital services. It should be noted, however, that some hospitals were signing up to report quality scores voluntarily, even before the MMA was passed. CMS announced in July 2003 a major initiative to propose the use of financial incentives "to encourage hospitals to provide high quality inpatient care."

As a start, CMS led off with the Physician Practice Group Demonstration Project, a pay-for-performance pilot program with 10 large physician group practices. The goal was to reward improvement in Medicare beneficiary outcomes by making additional 5-percent bonus payments for some chronic illnesses. As of Dec. 12, 2003, 2,338 hospitals had signed up with CMS to report their quality data. In 2005, MedPAC presented to Congress recommendations that would directly link part of Medicare's payment to providers—including inpatient hospitals—to performance.[3]

Another CMS initiative is the Premier Hospital Quality Incentive Demonstration, which is a national organization of about 1,500 nonprofit hospitals and health systems.[4] The voluntary project began in 2003, includes 268 member hospitals, and is designed to measure the effect of financial rewards or penalties on hospital care for some common medical conditions. The bonuses for performance in specific clinical areas (heart attack, heart failure, pneumonia, coronary artery bypass graft, and hip and knee replacements) are to be based on 34 nationally defined evidence-based, quality indicators as measured by the Agency for Healthcare Research and Quality (AHRQ), the Joint Commission on Accreditation of Healthcare Organizations (The Joint Commission), the National Quality Forum (NQF), the Ambulatory Care Quality Alliance (AQA), and other collaborators such as the American College of Surgeons National Surgical Quality Improvement Program (ACS NSQIP).

Results of CMS Program

As of late 2005, more than 270 hospitals nationwide were voluntarily taking part in a three-year demonstration project. Starting in the summer of 2005, the Premier Initiative has released results from the first 5 quarters showing a trend toward improved quality among all participants. In November 2005, CMS and the Premier demonstration project announced a bonus of $8.85 million as performance incentives for the top performing hospitals. For example, Hackensack University Medical Center in Newark, New Jersey, is projected to receive $326,000 for being a top performer in coronary artery bypass and $848,000 overall for all 5 clinical areas.[5] The project states that scores improved from 65 percent to 91 percent in clinical areas of acute myocardial infarction, heart failure, coronary artery bypass graft, pneumonia, and hip/knee replacements. The medical director of the partnership program between CMS and The Premier Initiative estimated that widespread utilization of the care measures, extrapolated to the nation, would have resulted in 3,000 fewer deaths, 6,000 fewer complications, and 500,000 fewer hospital days.

Objectives of Pay for Performance

Safavi observes that there are three basic goals of any program that seeks to link pay with performance:[6]

- Create a better payment system that is more fair;
- Align financial incentives with improved outcomes; and
- Encourage health care professionals to create added efficiency and stretch financial resources.

Pay-for-Performance Design

The Center for Studying Health System Change has summarized five mechanisms or designs that are being adopted for pay-for-performance programs:[7]

- Health care plans coalesce to coordinate payment to physician groups (Integrated Healthcare Association [IHA]);

- Employers pay individual physicians (Bridges to Excellence program);[8]

- Individual health plans pay physicians for performance (Medicare);

- Individual health plans pay physician groups for performance; and

- Physician groups pay individual physicians with no insurer involvement.

Incentives

The incentives of pay-for-performance programs typically include:[9]

- Annual bonuses for hospitals and physicians based on voluntary participation and meeting pre-agreed targets;

- Withholding a percentage of reimbursement that is paid back if targets are met;

- Retroactive adjustment of fee schedules; and

- Incentives created by employer coalitions.

The Advisory Board Company reports that the goal of improved clinical outcome and alignment with other initiatives were the health plans' top reasons for initiating programs. Interestingly, employer pressures and improved medical loss ratio (percentage of insurance premiums spent on providing care) and, therefore, lower costs were least important.[10]

MedPAC recommended setting aside 1 percent to 2 percent of hospital payments to create a pool for rewarding quality performance. HHS would then establish regulations. Two-percent bonuses would be awarded to the top 10 percent of the hospitals for demonstrating performance and improvement over a period of time depending on their base diagnosis-related group (DRG) payments for the clinical condition. A 1-percent bonus would be awarded to the next 10 percent of performing hospitals. A 2-percent reduction would be in place for those hospitals below the 10-percent baseline during the third year of the project for the clinical DRGs being reviewed. A 1-percent penalty would be levied on those institutions between 10 percent and 20 percent below the baseline.

National Private Insurer Experience

Private groups such as IHA in California,[11] whose members include seven of the largest health plans (covering 85 percent of California's

10 million commercial health maintenance organization [HMO] enrollees), have pushed to measure performance based on clinical quality, patient experience, and investment in information technology. The IHA is a nonprofit, statewide health care leadership group composed of representatives from all stakeholders that have had a pay-for-performance program for 5 years. It recently reported findings involving 225 physician groups representing approximately 35,000 doctors caring for 6.2 million HMO patients in California. Clinical results improved from 1 percent to 10 percent for 2003–2004 for all measures during the 2 years for which performance was analyzed.[12] For the 2 years, based on meeting performance targets, physician groups received a combined total of approximately $90 million in 2003–2004 pay-for-performance–related bonus payments from 7 participating health plans.

Med-Vantage, a company that consults on pay-for-performance issues, reported that active pay-for-performance programs were increased from 84 in 2004 to 107 in 2005. These programs covered more than 50 million enrolled lives and were projected to reach 160 programs in 2006.[10] Pay for performance was implemented in 73 commercial health plans, 13 Medicaid plans, 8 government agencies, and 6 other programs. Med-Vantage also reported that only 38 percent of these entities assessed the potential impact on clinical outcome, and only 26 percent had any idea of return on investment before rolling out their pay-for-performance programs.

The Blue Cross and Blue Shield Association reports a larger number of plans proceeding with implementation of pay-for-performance programs. The usual progression has been to set goals, gradually switch from partial payment based on achieving goals, and ultimately tie a significant percentage of payment to meeting well-demonstrated quality indicators.

Bridges to Excellence is a nonprofit coalition of insurers, providers, and employers that, in cooperation with the American Board of Internal Medicine, has announced a program that could provide cash incentives to primary care physicians. The initiative was announced at a national pay-for-performance summit sponsored by IHA.[8] The initiative is also intended to build some support among solo and small practices that do not have adequate resources to comply with reporting standards.[13]

Early Results

From an individual physician's perspective, the program involves a financial cost to track the quality indicators, demonstrate results, and be eligible for extra payments. Physician groups are asking for a commitment of new dollars up-front to fund data-entry systems to achieve the goals of a pay-for-performance program. It is estimated that the cost of an electronic medical record system is about $5,000 per physician annually in addition to the initial capital outlay. Physicians are concerned about consultants being paid to "game" the system for bonuses, rather than actual improvement in patient care.

Will pay-for-performance programs truly change delivery of care, or reward large, well-capitalized and already well-performing organizations that possess the tools to gather and measure performance? The Commonwealth Fund supported a study by Rosenthal and others who evaluated a pay-for-performance program by reviewing quality improvement reports issued to 2 different health care groups encompassing 300 large physician organizations.[14] The program measured cervical cancer screening, mammography, and hemoglobin A_{1C} over a 3-year period. The conclusion: 75 percent of incentive payments went to already well-performing groups that recognized they simply needed to maintain the status quo.

Position of Organized Medicine

Leading organizations in health care have issued statements to explain their stand on the pay-for-performance programs. These include the Medical Group Management Association (MGMA),[15] American Medical Association (AMA),[16] American Academy of Family Physicians,[17] American College of Physicians (ACP),[18] and American College of Surgeons (ACS).[19]

MGMA in a position paper [15] has outlined principles that can help physicians and managers evaluate the foundation of any pay-for-performance program. These are:

- Patient care and safety should the primary goal;

- Physicians and their management and organizations must be involved in the design of these programs;

- Participation must be voluntary;

- Measures used to gauge quality must be supported by generally accepted scientific evidence and risk adjusted for variations in patient populations;

- Cost of participation must be covered by compensation or other financial rewards; and

- Artificial volume control formulas, such as the sustainable growth rate (SGR) formula (used by Medicare) to determine reimbursement, must be avoided.

MedPAC, the congressional commission charged with recommending payment reforms, has suggested starting with 1 percent to 2 percent of Medicare payments placed in an incentive pool.[20] Several professional organizations (AMA, ACP, MGMA, and ACS) have objected to the budget neutral payment stance of MedPAC. The ACP argues that organizational rewards for reducing hospitalizations and emergency room admissions, which are largely due to physician efforts, should be shared with physicians.

There is some disagreement within organized medicine as jockeying for an advantage occurs based on which physician group translates the pay-for-performance project into economic benefit for its members. In his inaugural address to the AMA, William Pested, the organization's then-incoming president stated, "Most pay-for-performance programs amount to little more than arrogantly blatant excuses to reduce payments to the majority of physicians."[21] However, in December 2005, the AMA announced that it had reached a working agreement with Congress. It would develop 140 measures of quality in 34 clinical areas to allow physicians to voluntarily report their performance to the federal government by the end of 2007.[22] In opposition to the AMA, several specialty societies, including the Alliance of Specialty Medicine, which represents 13 medical-specialty societies with a total of more than 200,000 physicians, criticized the secret deal. They said the plan was far too complicated, that it was brokered without comment from the specialty societies, and that the AMA was designating itself as the sole representative of physicians whose interests may not be in line with the AMA.

The Surgical Care Improvement Project (SCIP), a national partnership of organizations, was established by CMS and CDC with the goal of reducing postoperative mortality and morbidity by 25 percent over the next 5 years.[23] The SCIP program is a national project with 10 collaborating organizations including CMS, AHA, AHRQ, and the Joint Commission. Another group representing primary care practitioners is proceeding with a 3-year pilot program called "Improving Performance in Practice" involving 100 physicians in Colorado and North Carolina who will receive assistance in collecting and reporting on diabetes and asthma.[24]

Patient Perspective

Consumer-driven health care is a common buzzword implying that better informed consumers will make their own decisions regarding their health issues, resulting in demand for higher quality care at competitive prices. Consumers are just starting to have gross hospital and physician performance data available, and the anticipation is that the consumers want and will have information that will help them make better choices, reward better quality providers, and drive business away from poor performers. While pay for performance is getting the attention of health policy experts and insurers, the common person does not yet appear to be willing to pay higher premiums for better quality health care.

A *Wall Street Journal Online*/Harris Interactive poll of 2,123 adults in April 2006 shows that 33 percent of all U.S. adults are in favor of health insurance plans tying payment to quality of care (44 percent in 2003); however, the number of adults who remain unsure about the issue has increased from 40 percent in 2003 to 54 percent in 2006.[25] Most adults (57 percent) also said they would *not* be willing to pay a significantly larger premium for physicians and hospitals who have demonstrated better quality health care. Based on the survey, patients seem to recognize the fairness of having quality indicators, but do not want to pay higher premiums for better quality care and do not seem to want their own physician's payments tied to quality of care.

Patient satisfaction surveys are also being considered in any formula to pay for health care. Rochester Independent Practice Association uses patient satisfaction surveys to compensate physicians for up to 20 percent of pay. Similarly, Tufts Health Plan in Massachusetts used patient satisfaction ratings to withhold bonuses from 3,000 to 4,000 physicians. A former president of the California Medical Association is quoted as stating that 8 of the largest insurers in California use the program to distribute $30 million among 35,000 physicians based on patient satisfaction scores, often paying bonuses of up to $5,000 to individual physicians.[26] California's Office of the Patient Advocate displays ratings for HMOs and some HMO physician groups.[27]

Unanswered Questions

Opelka and Brown pose a fundamental question: Is health care a commodity?[28] They argue that if it is a commodity, then cost alone should be the final determining factor in the reimbursement process. Most consumers and health care professionals will concede that quality of care is the more important factor. The underlying basis for altering incentives starts with accurately measuring performance. Landon and colleagues have attempted to assess the future of these tools and point to the lack of evidence-based measures.[29]

There are more questions than there are answers at this time. Physicians and medical managers have seen many such initiatives come, and then rapidly fizzle out after an initial flurry of activity. Some important questions that need to be answered prior to large-scale adoption of pay for performance are:

- What happens when the poor quality providers of care, and the only ones in their communities, have been weeded out?

- What happens when most institutions have learned to "game" the system through a better selection of patients within the clinical groups being studied and rejecting high-risk patients?

Unless there is a perfectly validated weighting system for the sickest patients, tying financial incentives to payment is likely to reward institutions and physicians for reporting the best results in patients selected on the basis of their risk factors and severity of illness. Pricewaterhouse Coopers reports that 85 percent of organizations surveyed are moving toward some type of pay-for-performance initiative.[30] Ultimately, there is the potential that any pay-for-performance program could be seen as arbitrary and not predictive of high-quality care; rather than creating a culture of quality, pay for performance could lead to misreporting driven primarily by bonus payments. Such developments could lead to the unintended consequence of hospitals narrowly focusing their interventions at the expense of broadly improving care.[31,32] The entire focus from a physician perspective is to reward physicians for demonstrating quality care by paying them bonuses as well as publicizing their score cards and driving more patients to their practices.

There are potential traps for physicians. Not all physicians will agree on what criteria are scientifically valid, or how to adjust for high-risk patients. A consequence could be that practices avoid taking care of high-risk patients or figure out how to "game" the system. Questions to consider include:

- What happens if providing the best care actually raises the cost of health care? It is evident that no payer will come up with additional funds for bonuses, but will try to either cut costs or at the worst, remain budget neutral. Most physicians suspect that some insurers' sole purpose is to decrease their medical loss ratio (percentage of dollars actually spent on medical care vs. administrative or other costs) under the guise of improving quality of care;

- Will payers be risk averse and keep bonus payments to 1 percent to 2 percent, in which case there may not be enough incentive for hospitals to spend millions of dollars in information technology and software?

- Will the current anti-kickback and Stark laws be modified, or exceptions created to allow hospitals to assist physicians in being able to afford systems to collect, maintain and report quality indicators?

- How much will the effort cost and who will pay for it?

- If electronic medical records are part of the equation, how will small practices pay for the investment and will the payoff be enough to cover the costs of the technology?

- What happens when the payers keep raising the bar? Highmark Blue Cross/Blue Shield in western Pennsylvania was so successful in meeting set targets in 2004 that it raised the bar for bonus payments.[33]

Information technology that allows insurers, health care organizations, and physicians to collect, compare, and report key indicators of quality is expected to play a major role in this effort. Institutions and physician groups may be able to demonstrate improved outcomes, but could be left out of the bonus pool if they are not in the top 20 percent of performers, as an example, and have to absorb the cost of implementation.

The Leapfrog Group has designed a "turnkey" measure that hospitals can use based on the Premier project.[9] The Rewards Program, a nationally standardized program that can be licensed to allow employers and health plans to track performance in 5 clinical areas representing 20 percent of commercial inpatient spending and 33 percent of commercial admissions, will recognize and reward hospitals for their performance in both the quality and efficiency of inpatient care.

Future Directions

Gail Wilensky, a previous CMS administrator, has stated that the ultimate goal is to reward health care organizations and practitioners that "do it well, do it right, and do it efficiently."[34] It is clear that physicians do not want to be stuck with the costs of implementation in addition to a zero-sum eventuality such as the SGR formula. *Medical Economics* conducted a survey designed to gauge the influence of pay-for-performance programs on office-based physicians in 23 specialties.[35] Twenty four percent of all respondents and 30 percent of primary care physicians indicated that at least one health plan they contracted with offered pay for performance. The employers desperately want to see an end in sight for escalation of health care costs, but do not want to front the expenses for the technology. The insurance companies are anxious to have more control over rewards and penalties, but without hurting their profit margins. Employer-driven initiatives, such as the Leapfrog Group, have partnered with Med-Vantage to cooperate in a national survey to track all incentive and pay-for-performance programs. Large insurers, such as CIGNA, have agreed to share claims data with the Leapfrog Group and Bridges to Excellence to achieve better efficiency.[9]

Consumer advocates would like to see more transparency in pricing and quality outcomes, but at no added expense. As part of the overall program, consumers will be offered even more incentives to take advantage of preventive care services, risk-reducing habits, and lower premiums for better behavior. However, they may be required to participate in health risk assessment.

The government is in the role of leading a charge and attempting to herd various factions together and set some general rules. Even though the House–Senate conference in December 2005 left pay for performance out of the budget reconciliation package, it is clear that CMS and private payers are making the logical assumption that poor care results in complications that raise costs, and good quality care leads to lower costs. They see the pay-for-performance initiative as one of the major ways to decrease costs by forcing hospitals and physicians to collect, report, and be paid for providing better care, rather than getting paid regardless of outcomes. After CMS has consensus through various third-party intermediaries (including AMA, NQF, AQA, and the ACS NSQIP), it will likely seek help in using "G-codes," which are descriptors of services reported along with CPT® procedure codes. Once the collected information has been analyzed, CMS will more than likely push for robust pay-for-performance measures.

A survey of chief executive officers indicates that payers' implementation of pay-for-performance contracts with hospitals based on cost or quality are very likely or somewhat likely in 72 percent and 91 percent, respectively.[36] Umbdenstock, citing the same survey, reports that health care executives also believe it is very likely or somewhat likely that hospitals will be forced to disclose price (89 percent) and quality (99 percent) information.[37]

As health plans, employers, and government agencies grapple with health care costs, anything that has even a glimmer of hope is hailed as the solution. Safavi points out three main issues that are at the core of arguments between those providing the care and those paying for it.[38] First is the payer's premise that the double-digit growth in cost is partially due to rewards for more medical activity and, to cut spending, the incentives have to change. This assumes that doing less will improve the quality of care. Physicians have to assume that payers want a net decrease in their expenses (and an increase in their profits), and that improving quality is simply a way to pay less for services. Second, Safavi correctly observes that the Medicare pay-for-performance, for example, rewards the entire system and not individual performers and conflicts with the gainsharing concept, which holds the individual accountable. Finally, will financial incentives change the usual way performance is measured, such as death and complication rates?

Like many high-profile policy initiatives, pay for performance has generated a lot of attention because it is seen as a vehicle that may result in the "Holy Grail:" cost restraint and improved quality of care at the same time. The future of pay for performance is by no means certain.

References

1. H. Gleckman, *Business Week*, Oct. 10, 2005, 101–102.

2. Institute of Medicine, "Redesigning Health Insurance Performance Measures, Payment, and Performance Improvement Programs, www.iom.edu/CMS/3809/19805.aspx (accessed Feb. 20, 2006).

3. D.O. Weber, "Pay-For-Performance Programs Pressure and Please Physicians," *The Physician Executive,* May–June, 2006, 6–11.

4. Centers for Medicare and Medicaid Services, "Hospital Quality Alliance," www.cms.hhs.gov/HospitalQualityInits/15_Hospital QualityAlliance.asp (accessed June 24, 2006).

5. M. Hagland, "Pay for Performance Programs Show Results, Spur Development, *Health Care Strategic Mgmt* 24 (2) (2006): 1–3.

6. K. Safavi, "Aligning Financial Incentives," *J Healthcare Mgmt* 51 (3) (2006): 146–151.

7. T. Bodenheimer, and others, "Can Money Buy Quality? Physician Response to Pay for Performance," *Issue Brief No. 102*, December 2005, Robert Wood Johnson Foundation, www.rwjf.org/pr/index.jsp (accessed July 4, 2006).

8. Bridges to Excellence, "Press Release: GE, Ford, UPS, P&G< Verizon, Others Back New Pay-For-Quality Initiative, for Physicians," April 10, 2003, www.bridgestoexcellence.org/bte/bte_ pressrelease_1.htm.

9. The Leapfrog Group, www.leapfroggroup.org/media/file/ LeapfrogPay_for_Performance_Briefing.pdf (accessed Feb. 20, 2006).

10. The Advisory Board Company, "Innovations Center, Health Care Advisory Board: Pay For Performance: How Far, How Fast?" www.advisory.com (accessed Feb. 20, 2006).

11. Integrated Healthcare Association, www.iha.org/Ihaproj.htm (accessed June 29, 2006).

12. Integrated Healthcare Association, "Integrated Healthcare Association Shares Five Years of Experience in Pay for Performance with Healthcare Leaders at National Conference," Feb. 6, 2006, www.iha.org/020606.htm (accessed June 29, 2006).

13. M. Romano, "Bridging a Quality Movement: Collaboration Seeks to Make Pay-For-Performance a Mainstream Practice," *Modern Healthcare* Feb. 13, 2006, 14–15.

14. The Commonwealth Fund, "Early Experience with Pay-for-Performance: From Concept to Practice," www.cmwf.org/publications/publications_show.htm?doc_id=307183 (accessed Feb. 13, 2006).

15. Medical Group Management Association, "Principles for Pay-for-Performance Programs and Recommendations for Medical Group Practices," February 2005, www.mgma.com/WorkArea/showcontent.aspx?id=1454 (accessed Feb. 10, 2006).

16. American Medical Association, www.ama-assn.org.

17. American Academy of Family Physicians, "Pay-for-Performance," www.aafp.org/online/en/home/policy/policies/p/payforperformance.html (accessed June 29, 2006).

18. American College of Physicians, www.acponline.org.

19. American College of Surgeons, www.facs.org.

20. Medicare Payment Advisory Commission, *Report to the Congress: Medicare Payment Policy.* Washington, D.C.: MedPAC (March 2005).

21. "Outliers, Asides, and Insides" *Modern Healthcare* 36 (25) (2006): 64.

22. D. Glendinning. "AMA Leads Project to Develop Quality Measures by Year's End," *AMNews* (March 13, 2006), www.ama-assn.org/amednews/2006/03/13/gvl10313.htm (accessed March 6, 2007).

23. MedQIX, Medicare Quality Improvement Community, www.medqic.org (accessed July 3, 2006).

24. M. Romano, "Medical Groups Collaborate on Pay-for-Performance Pilot," *Modern Health Care,* May 15, 2006.

25. *The Wall Street Journal Online*/Harris Interactive, "Many U.S. Adults Believe Healthcare Quality Can Be Fairly Assessed, but Few Willing to Pay Significantly Higher Premiums for Superior Care," *The Wall Street Journal Online*, April 4, 2006, www.harrisinteractive.com/news/newsletters/wsjhealthnews/WSJOnline_HI_Health-CarePoll2006vol5_iss06.pdf (accessed May 1, 2006).

26. G. Kolata, "When the Doctor Is In, but You Wish He Weren't," *New York Times,* Nov. 30, 2005 (Correction Dec. 2, 2005) www.nytimes.com/2005/11/30/health/30patient.html?pagewanted=1&ei=5070&en=72e6963fb35f904e&ex=1177646400 (accessed April 23, 2007).

27. Office of the Patient Advocate, "Report Cards," State of California, www.opa.ca.gov/reports/#rc (accessed Feb. 20, 2006).

28. F.G. Opelka and C.A. Brown, "Understanding Pay for Performance," *Bull Am Coll Surg,* 90 (9) (2005): 12–17.

29. B.E. Landon, and others, "Physician Clinical Performance Assessment: Prospects and Barriers," *JAMA* 290 (9) (2003): 1183–1189.

30. T. Walker, "Proactive Leaders Thrive in Competitive Climate," *Managed Healthcare Executive* 16 (2) (2006): 8–9.

31. C.N. Kahn, and others, "Snapshot of Hospital Quality Reporting and Pay-for-Performance Under Medicare," *Health Affairs* 25 (1) (2006): 148–163.

32. M.B. Rosenthal, and others, "Early Experience with Pay-for-Performance," *JAMA* 294 (14) (2005): 1788–93.

33. The Advisory Board Company, www.advisoryboard.com (accessed June 20, 2006).

34. G. Wilensky, "On the Road to a National Performance Measurement System," *Healthcare Finan Mgmt* 60 (2) (2006): 46–47.

35. K. Terry, "Pay for Performance: How Fast Is It Spreading?" *Medical Economics* 82 (21) (2005): 30.

36. R.L. Clarke, "Payment: Performance Payment Proliferates," *Futurescan: Healthcare Trends and Implications 2006–2011.* Chicago: American College of Healthcare Executives Health Administration Press (2006): 25–28.

37. R.J. Umbdenstock, "Health Policy: After Katrina, A Whole New Ballgame," *Futurescan: Healthcare Trends and Implications 2006-2011.*

Chicago: American College of Healthcare Executives Health Administration Press (2006): 9–12.

38. K. Safavi, "Pay for Performance: Finding Common Ground," *J Healthcare Mgmt* 51 (1) (2006): 9–12.

About the Author

Bhagwan Satiani, MD, MBA, FACS, is a professor of clinical surgery in the Division of Vascular Surgery, and medical director of the Non-Invasive Vascular Laboratory at The Ohio State University College of Medicine in Columbus. He is also president of Savvy Medicine, a physician-led organization that educates health care practitioners on business-related topics. He has practiced vascular surgery since 1978. Dr. Satiani's additional professional interests include coordinating business education seminars for physicians and practice management seminars for surgical residents. He also developed an 18-month curriculum for surgical residents in the Department of Surgery to prepare them for the economic, legal, and personal finance challenges ahead of them. Married for 36 years and the father of two children, Dr. Satiani's numerous community interests include volunteering for ASHA—Ray of Hope, a Columbus, Ohio organization to prevent domestic violence in South Asians. He also plays percussion in an Indian music group in Columbus.

About the Contributors

Rebecca Dawson, CPC, is compliance specialist at OSU Physicians, Inc., in Columbus, Ohio. (Chapter 4: Getting Paid, Part 1: Introduction to Coding and the Global Surgery Package)

E. Ann Gabriel, PhD, CPA, is assistant professor, School of Accountancy, Ohio University, in Athens, Ohio. (Chapter 6: Financial Statements: What They Are and What They Tell Us; Chapter 7: Using Financial Statements to Make Decisions)

Ray Manley, CMPE, is clinical assistant professor of surgery, chief operating officer, OSU Surgery LLC, Department of Surgery at The Ohio State University School of Medicine in Columbus, Ohio. (Chapter 1: The Revenue Cycle)

Index